Pay It Forward Series

# Notes to My

# Younger Self

*– Volume 3 –*

## By Kezia Luckett

The Pay it Forward: Notes to My Younger Self
Volume 3

First Printed in United Kingdom 2020

Published by Women of Contribution Global Publishing
*www.womenofcontribution.com*

ISBN: 978-1-9163443-0-3

# Praise for Notes to My Younger Self

Every chapter in the *Pay It Forward* series gives you the ability to see how resilient women are and their capability to overcome any obstacle. This book will help you recognise and acknowledge the transformation women are going through collectively. No woman is an island – together we rock.

*Kay Newton – the mid-life strategist*

The gems of wisdom, insight and advice from each woman's story not only demonstrate courage and vulnerability in sharing the healing process of her journey, but are inspiring and uplifting to the reader. The women's stories in the Notes to My Younger Self series reveal the truth that we are all connected by experiencing the same emotions and feelings; and yet reflects the resilience, strength, and beauty of unique souls sharing this human experience. A truly life-changing gift; thank you.

*Claire Rowlands – spiritual creative and healer*

I'm so glad I had the opportunity to read and review this book. When we are younger, and going through all that life throws at us, we don't know the possibilities, but the idea of going back and sharing our knowledge with our younger self helps us realise how far we've come. I found myself caring for and cheering on these women, knowing they will evolve and grow and gain the confidence they need to live the life they deserve. Reading the stories of these young women helped me realise the strength I have in me too because of all my past experiences. It makes life less scary and helps open up the world of possibilities. As Monica Cor Auri says, "There is a difference between strength and force". Rather than forcing through, we call on our strength to guide us and know we are equipped to move through life with strength and grace. After reading these stories, it is clear these women are a strength to be reckoned with.

*Jen Frost – goals and success coach*

Each of the women who share their story in this volume also share a part of our collective self. We feel the hurt they describe because it taps into the hurt we have inside our own soul. Though one letter describes a literal moment, we have all held a proverbial knife to our throat in some way. We may not have pushed cold steel to our neck, but we have sliced the voice of our emotions and desires and compromised for various reasons. Everyone has a story; and we each can relate on some level. Whether we are just starting out and want to know that someone else has made it through the hopeless moments or we have conquered our biggest demons and are looking back on our journey, we know these women's stories in ourselves. This book not only shares stories of specific women on the surface, but also each letter shares a piece of our own story that we recognise in others. This collection summons each of us to rise to our power!

*Tiffany Brix – wellness coach and freelance writer*

Another wonderful collection of inspiring ladies to read about. Often we see success stories and, while it's wonderful to see people doing well, it can seem out of reach and unrelatable. We may assume, "but they've not had to go through the things I have," but these women bravely open up and show us the hurdles they have overcome in life and how each obstacle has helped them eventually bloom and grow. It's a wonderful book to show that we are all capable of reaching for the stars. A real inspiration for us all, no matter what life has been like so far.

*Claire Gibbs*

# Dedication

This book is dedicated to every woman who has been told she is too much, too little, too fat, or too thin.

For every woman who has dimmed down, stepped back, been criticised, ridiculed or teased.

For every woman who has found themselves in difficult situations, with no easy way out.

For every woman who has found herself defined by her looks, the shape of her body, the size of her breasts, the tilt of her nose or the clothes on her back.

For every woman who has been judged for her quietness, her loudness, her opinions and her sexuality.

For every woman who is suffering with her mental health or an unseen condition or illness.

For every woman who second-guesses everything she does, as the negative monkey chatter starts to take over and threatens to throw her off the rails.

This book is for EVERY WOMAN.

Regardless of where you have come from, where you are going, or what your experience has been in between, this is for you to know your time has now come to share, support and encourage other women from around the globe that they are enough, and always have been.

# Contents

# Your Turn to Pay It Forward

In your hands you hold a book containing a wealth of hope, wisdom, knowledge and inspiration gained through the experiences of life.

To truly understand the power of the written word and what happens when women come together for a single cause, read the stories within these pages and, in the message box, write your own words of hope, wisdom, love and inspiration to the next woman you are going to pay the book forward to.

Give it to a friend, family member, or even a stranger by leaving it on a bus, train, park bench, or even on the table in your local cafe. If leaving for a stranger, place a Post-it note on the front and write: "Yes, this book is for you. Read it. Love it. Pay It Forward."

# Share Your Book & Pay it Forward:

Share a photo of you leaving or paying forward your book on social media on our official book page
*www.facebook.com/ThePayitForwardSeriesNotestoMyYoungerSelf*

Tag us in with these hashtags:
#womenofcontribution
#payitforward
#1billionlives
#aroundtheworld

Join us on our mission to positively impact on one billion lives because:
UNITED WE ARE STRONG
TOGETHER WE CAN MAKE A DIFFERENCE
ONE WOMAN AT A TIME

# Pay It Forward Messages

# Foreword

What do you tell the little girl who feels as though she's carrying the weight of the world on her shoulders? What do you tell the little girl who feels as though everyone has figured out how to be happy except for her? What do you tell the little girl who has a million deep questions that nobody seems to answer to her satisfaction?

From a very young age, I felt different. I was haunted by the history of human suffering I'd learnt of in school and perplexed by the meaning of life. While other kids were outside playing joyfully, I was grappling with inner sadness and depression.

But one summer day when I was twelve years old, I snuck into my older sister's bedroom to borrow a book to read while I sunbathed in our back yard. The book, *Siddhartha*, which was about the quest for enlightenment, showed me that I wasn't alone – that there were others in the world searching for answers like me.

A year later, my search led me to my first personal development workshop where I watched the great inspirational speaker, Zig Ziglar, and I made a commitment to myself to travel the world speaking and inspiring people. My quest continued and led me to learn meditation at age sixteen and become a meditation teacher at nineteen.

Since I wanted to stay grounded in what society would consider a traditional path, I got an MBA and became a top corporate executive.

I mixed that traditional path with the path of spirit, consulting with Vedic astrologers and using techniques like creative visualisation.

And this combination *seemed* to work. In my thirties and forties, if you had been looking at my life from the outside, you'd think I'd accomplished great success. I consulted in Fortune 500 companies, spoke to audiences of thousands around the world, and even became a #1 New *York Times* bestselling author many times over, selling more than sixteen million copies of my books.

But that did not satisfy the yearnings of my younger self. As my success grew, so did my dissatisfaction and unhappiness. Though I had accomplished most of my goals – a successful career, a nice home, a great life partner, wonderful friends – I still felt an emptiness inside.

So I searched more deeply to find the answers to true and lasting happiness, interviewing scientists and world-renowned experts along with unconditionally happy people. I applied what I learnt from all this research, and it worked – thankfully, I found answers to the questions I'd had as a child. My internal sadness and low-grade depression lifted and was replaced with a deep sense of fulfilment – what I call being "happy for no reason."

In reading the various stories in this book, you'll see how we're all searching for something. Whether you're yearning for acceptance, self-worth, meaning or forgiveness, your search will be fulfilled only when you listen to your own soul's wisdom and guidance, and you embrace your experiences in gratitude for the lessons they've taught you.

Writing back to your younger self, sharing the knowledge that you've gained over the years, is therapeutic and healing. You can see how each experience, adventure, high and low has shone light on your journey.

So, for my little girl who had so many questions when she was young, I want her to know that life can pan out. I'm grateful to report to her that it's actually worked out better than I could have imagined.

To all of our younger selves, please remember to tap into your inner knowing and follow your own soul's calling. It will not steer you wrong. I promise.

**Marci Shimoff**

#1 *New York Times* bestselling author, *Happy for No Reason* and *Chicken Soup for the Woman's Soul*. World-renowned transformational teacher and expert on happiness, success, and unconditional love.

*http://happyfornoreason.com/*

# Introduction

As many of us approach mid-life, the ideals and expectations of what we thought life would be at this age seem to clash with our reality. Looking in the mirror, it's hard to believe the woman staring back at us has been through everything she has.

On the outside she appears normal, with maybe a few more lines and wrinkles around her eyes and forehead than she had when she was younger, but on the inside her heart, thoughts, emotions and memories showcase the scars of: negative throwaway comments, expectations of others, failures, mistakes, loss, betrayal, isolation, loneliness, heartbreak and abuse.

Many of these experiences get hidden beneath the masks of "I'm fine," "life is good," "everything is all right," but recently women are realising the power that comes from exposing the raw, vulnerable side of their experience.

They know it is in the sharing with others that the first steps to healing can take place, that the shedding of what we have believed to be true, that we have allowed to define us, can be released and let go.

Writing a letter back to your younger self is part of a process each of our authors have gone through to experience their transformational change, and fill this wonderful book with stories that will help others.

On their journey to bring their stories to light, they have ridden the roller coaster of emotions and reassessed the memories they have cultivated and held dear to their hearts over the years. They have had difficult conversations with loved ones and been present with the person they once were and how this has shaped the person they now are.

Moving forward, they are clear on the power that each experience has had, course-correcting them over the years to be where they are now, fully embracing their true purpose on this planet and how they, individually and collectively, can send out positive ripples of change across the globe.

Having worked intensively with each woman, I am still in total awe of their courageousness, their giving hearts and their desire to make the world a better place for others. They are my true heroes in every sense of the word, and I know once you read their stories, they will be yours too.

But what I want you to remember as you read their stories and see the reflections in your own life, is that we all have the capability to change others' lives for the better, whether it is in sharing our stories, our smiles or our hearts, offering a listening ear, a shoulder to cry on or a place to retreat. Each of us are here for a purpose, and each of us can create a ripple of change for the better.

Discovering and knowing your purpose can send many women on a life-long hunt, but everything you ever wanted to know about your purpose is written in your past. In each experience you've had, with each person you've met, knowledge and wisdom has been gathered bringing you to this point.

The question NOW is whether you are ready to step forward? Whether you are ready to rise to the challenge of being visible, taking action and being recognised for the phenomenal woman of contribution you are?

This can often bring up feelings of fear, worry, and self-judgement. What will others think and say, and how can I change the world? But I want to remind you, in the words of Marianne Williamson:

*"Our deepest fear is not that we are inadequate. Our deepest fear is that we are powerful beyond measure. It is our light, not our darkness that most frightens us. We ask ourselves, 'Who am I to be brilliant, gorgeous, talented, fabulous?' Actually, who are you not to be? You are a child of God. You're playing small does not serve the world. There is nothing enlightened about shrinking so that other people won't feel insecure around you. We are all meant to shine, as children do. We were born to make manifest the glory of God that is within us. It's not just in some of us; it's in everyone. And as we let our own light shine, we unconsciously give other people permission to do the same. As we are liberated from our own fear, our presence automatically liberates others".*

You are meant to shine your light into the world and, just by being yourself, you CAN send out a ripple of change across the globe. This might sound like an easy thing to do, but so many women don't know who they are, and so many have forgotten the true essence of brilliance that lies within. They haven't been taught how to accept themselves without self-judgement, to honour themselves and what their bodies need without guilt, to respect themselves and listen to that inner whisper without fear of judgement.

Taking this journey to knowing ourselves can sometimes seem such a big task, with many women determining it's easier to do nothing at all, to carry on living a half-life and dying having never lived at all. But all the while you are not sharing yourself, your knowledge, wisdom and experience, another woman is falling, another woman is crying out for help, another woman is being taken advantage of.

Stepping forward and embracing your true power and brilliance doesn't have to be hard. Surrounding yourself with women, like-minded souls, who can comfort, support, accept and encourage you along the way not only makes it fun but removes the pressure of having to do it alone. This is why we created a like-minded community of women who are stepping forward to shine their light out into the world and get to know and love who they are. I would personally like to invite each of you to join our community at *https://www.readytorise.today* and discover a place of belonging, of connection, of transformational becoming and celebration, or join us at our Destined for Bigger Things – Women's Weekend Experience where you will discover where you belong, how to connect to yourself and others and how you can step up and contribute to the world *https://www.destinedforbiggerthings.com*

We all owe it to ourselves to put ourselves at the forefront of everything we do, not only for ourselves, but our daughters and sons, nieces and nephews, brothers and sisters, our friends and lovers. By demonstrating to the world, the importance of knowing, loving and caring for ourselves, we give permission to others to do the same.

It is my hope for you as you read the stories within these pages that you recognise the similarities in each of our journeys, and it gives you confidence to recognise that if these women can step forward to unite and change the world, you can too.

If you feel moved by these stories and are ready to become our next female leader of change, sharing your mission with the world, increasing your visibility and positioning yourself as an expert in your field, writing your story, join our **Female Leaders Mastermind programme** by applying here: *https://www. femaleleadersmastermind.com*

All my love, as always.

**Kezia xxxx**

---

**"Our life experiences enable us to grow in power, strength and wisdom. The stories that we have lived through can give us the courage to take action and realise our life purpose"**

– Monica Cor Auri –

---

# The Spiritual Wisdom of Opening Your Heart and Trusting Your Gut

### Monica Cor Auri

*Business wellbeing consultant and visionary spiritual guide*

What are you passionate about and how are you contributing to the world?

Over the last twenty years I've inspired thousands of driven and disruptive leaders and professionals to take stock, make time to recover, find purpose and thrive after challenge, loss or life change.

I believe that wellbeing and practical spirituality are the foundation for happiness, growth and success. I'm passionate about helping people to be physically well, release emotional baggage, get mental clarity and access spiritual comfort through all stages of life. I do this by providing well-being mentoring, spiritual guidance, ceremony, nurturing support and kick-ass accountability for those who are called to work with me.

My vision is to inspire at least 800 million people to be successful, abundant and impactful at home and work by collaborating with others through Business Wellbeing® Global and my podcast, *The Spiritual Kitchen.*

**Describe a pivotal time in your life you would like to share.**
Imagine in front of you a Russian doll. You know, the type of wooden doll you split in half to find smaller and smaller versions of the same core figure until you get to the tiny one at the centre.

As you get a stronger image of that doll, notice she's wearing vibrant, beautiful clothing, a headdress and has a shiny, smiling, ebony face.

The seam between her two halves rests between her heart and her abdomen, her womb and her guts. To open her, the top and bottom halves of the doll are twisted in opposite directions to reveal another version inside with a deeper story to tell.

This largest version of the wooden doll that you see is me at the point where I have received the invitation to write this letter to my younger self. I'm writing this letter to the next-largest version inside.

To open up to a previous version, there is a spiritual awakening; an insight into the sacred creativity of life that requires a pivotal moment to wake us and force us to listen.

You see, my note begins with a life and death moment at the age of forty-three. This is the point where this version of Monica is finally able to listen to all the messages she has been given before. This version of Monica is wearing a hospital gown and I'm writing to ask her to wake up and get clear about the life she is here to live. I am inviting her to see that the seeds planted to get her to that place of depletion and illness were planted long ago.

As a result of listening to the wisdom revealed in the letter, we're able to open up the heart and trust the guts to reveal the forty-year-old version of Monica having a mid-life crisis, throwing out old ways of working, shining brightly though feeling brittle and dry inside without the courage to move, even though she knows she has to.

We can open up this version of the doll to reveal the thirty-six-year-old version of Monica having had a complete physical, emotional, mental and spiritual breakdown and breakthrough. Feeling the weight of deep grief after miscarriages and four failed rounds of IVF. Buckling under the weight of responsibility and the need to meet others' expectations of what it means to be a woman and mother.

The spiritual twist reveals another version of the thirty-two-year-old Monica devastated by the death of her soul sister, Susan. Feeling into the pain and the promise that she has been asked as a dying wish to make sure she fulfils her purpose and lives her dreams.

The previous version is revealed at a point where Monica was broken in half by a near-death experience. We see the twenty-three-year-old version of Monica pushing and pushing to train for the marathon, to fast track to professional excellence while being bullied and stalked, collapsing and losing her memory from pure exhaustion.

The spiritual insight continues to open up to another previous major version of Monica, to reveal the seventeen-year-old clinging to her first love. We watch how the fear of abandonment feeds into the actions of this young woman, prompting her to search for security in all the wrong places and make vows to keep everything together, come what may.

Open her up to reveal the eleven-year-old Monica wrestling with the break-up of her parents, trying to cope with witnessing the loss and confusion of the adults she was looking up to for guidance and clarity. Finding places of refuge, solace and secrecy under the radar of her father and holding her painful experiences and fear inside so as not to burden others.

Open her up to find the six-year-old version of Monica stating very clearly, but in hushed tones, that she didn't want to have children, after hearing the message over and over again that being a woman is a curse, being a girl is not as valuable as being a boy, being a mother is a burden and a weight that is heavy and miserable to bear.

Open her up to the next version of Monica. We reveal the four-year-old who was told to stop dancing, to stop being so provocative as it would get her into trouble. The one who shut down her radiant goddessness, her love of her body and connection with it to please others, to shut out the feeling that somehow she'd caused herself to be touched in a way she didn't want to be touched.

The last wave of awakening comes to reveal the smallest version of Monica. She is the baby Monica in the womb. Arriving early after swimming in the painful, toxic waters already carrying the chains of her ancestors and her family, knowing that at some level she needed to come through to enable herself and those around her to release those shackles, break the chains, move forward with gratitude, appreciation, hope and love rather than guilt, fear and obligation.

And so it is that we come to this point where we put the smaller versions of Monica back into a single whole, a complete and vibrant woman who is more than all of the parts that have been acknowledged, spoken and unspoken. We put her back together. We learn from the patterns and beliefs. We accumulate the truth, wisdom and strength that emanates from it all.

It is from this point that I write this letter back to my younger self to acknowledge all that has gone before, and as a prompt to move forward, to honour the truth of my existence, my strength, power and purpose. And yours.

**Based on the wealth of knowledge, wisdom and experience you have now, what would you like to say to yourself back then?**

*Your body is shutting down, Monica. This is your choice. Stay or go. Let go of this body and start again, in another lifetime perhaps, or stay, recover and do what you're meant to do in this body, this time.*

*You've been courageous before, you can do it again. And this time, now you have the insight, take action. Let go of everything that has run its course.*

*Be compassionate, have integrity, and take action. All that you want wants you.*

*You just have to claim it and make space for it in your life.*

*If we look back together, you can see all of the events that have brought you to this moment so that you can realise what you're here for and make the choice to move forward, step in or out. Clinically what has brought you here, they say, are the adhesions from the previous operation you had ten years ago; they wrapped around your small intestine, causing parts of it to die. They say it's your womb growing fibroids that cause pressure in your abdomen. They say this is the end of your fertility journey, and you'll be coming out of the operation without your womb, with your small intestine and bowels removed, a stoma and a colostomy bag.*

*The shit is about to hit the fan.*

*It's clear you couldn't stomach the situation any more. Your body has said, "Enough." You've tied yourself up in knots thinking about the situation of leaving your husband, of starting anew. You really don't like letting go, do you?*

*It's all about this relationship, this tied-up, bound, co-dependent relationship with your husband, your unwillingness to let go, your determination to make it work no matter what, even if it causes your death.*

*The physical root of this started in the decision to have your fibroids surgically removed after your body, with enough fibroids to grow it to the size of twenty-eight-week pregnancy, managed to produce something the size of a small pineapple or grapefruit and a couple of small oranges as benign tumours growing inside you. You've been a prize champion in growing fibroids.*

*But they're benign; we can't blame the fibroids. The fibroids have been diligently swallowing up the spare hormones, the toxic thoughts, feelings and behaviours, the incongruence of the life you've been living. Your womb has saved you, Monica, and now it's time for you to save your womb again. Reclaim the seat of your creativity, freedom and joy, and claim it back. Take back your sovereignty, the strength you willingly abdicated within your marriage.*

*You've been awesome at holding on to your pain and the pain of others, swallowing grief and using your womb and guts as a toxic dumping ground. Now you need to use that massive heart of yours to become a gold medallist at acknowledging your feelings, taking the right action and letting go of all that holds you back. This is how you will serve others fully.*

*Your soon-to-be-ex-husband is a good man in his own right. He's just not for you any more. Be grateful for how much you have grown together. Yet, recognise you've striven to keep it together long past its 'Best Before date'. That is not good for either of you and now it's time to let go.*

*The fact you were at moments during this illness vomiting bile and having a tube running through the back of your mouth and nose, where the faecal matter was coming out of your mouth and guts but the wrong way, literally means this situation stinks, and it has to go. It's time to let go. Let go, please.*

*It's time to make the decision to take action to move into the truth of who you are and what you bring. Heed your own message. You've been teaching this stuff for a long time. We teach what we most need to know and apply; knowledge is a burden unless it is applied.*

*The last time, your body gave you this warning by growing the huge fibroids. Remember the feeling you had after your operation, during recovery, that you needed to leave and start again, that this was a new start, an opportunity to leave whole, well, happy, and rested. Why did you stay? Fear.*

*You stayed because you were afraid to take action, not because you didn't know. You stayed because you valued loyalty and togetherness more than your sanity and felt the fallout would be too great. You also stayed to have a baby, but you were not with the right man who wanted a baby with you. You believed you were too old to find someone else, and the thought of going back on your word or letting go was completely unpalatable because, again, you were going to keep this together no matter what. Now you know better.*

*You were also given this opportunity in 2011 when you had your breakdown. Yes, the message was clear then, wasn't it, also? "Leave and start again. This situation is stifling you, and although you love him and respect him as a friend, this is co-dependence and you need to leave." But you kept it together at all costs.*

*You even had the message when you had your near-death experience back in 2001! You collapsed with oxygen depletion during a race. Running, running, running, striving, striving, striving, ready to run a marathon; pushing, pushing, pushing. There's a difference between strength and force, and you've been using force all these years to try to make this happen when, actually, by taking the right action, it could have been easy for you.*

*You chose to ignore these messages, not trust your inner wisdom, and even when you had the insights, you forgot to use and take the opportunity to make the different choices you could have made. You could have had the life you want. You can have what you want, but you have to break the chains of the past; unshackle yourself from the voluntary and involuntary bonds that have wrapped you and held you back.*

*Your body has not been working against you. She's always been on your side. She's just getting you to see that something is wrong, and if you think about the fibroids and this pattern, this is coming from your ancestors. Think of your ancestors when they were slaves, and they had no choice over their reproduction; they were raped, subjected to horrendous situations you didn't even want to comprehend. What could your ancestors do to their bodies do to prevent these unwanted pregnancies, or to prevent their precious children being born into slavery?*

*What they could do is produce fibroids to make a physical barrier to the heartbreak, the emotional, mental and spiritual dilemma. This is what it feels like to you, that you've been shackled, and you haven't found a safe, free space to allow your womb to receive the seed for you to become a mother. Your infertility story isn't even your story, your stuff. It's your mother's stuff, your ancestors' stuff. Knowing that your mother also got into a situation where she no longer wanted to have children but was having them, and that started with you. She didn't really want you.*

*It's necessary to clear this feeling. You need to make peace with this, to clear this legacy of enslavement. It's time to do that now. It is time to make peace, to heal, to know you are no longer a slave and you have choice, and all that come after you, all of your family who connected with you and this energy and this space, are also free. Free to choose.*

*If you have a deep emotion that runs through you, it's fear, the fear of abandonment. Sitting in this hospital bed now, be aware of it. This is also ancestral. This was the start of your mother and father's story. They were both abandoned by their mothers. This happened to your brothers and sisters and to you, too, when your mother left you to move to Barbados when you were eleven. This fear of abandonment also prompts you to cling on where otherwise it would be better for you to let go. Remember, the universal mother is always here supporting you, loving you, holding you. And the physical mother will always abandon you, even if she loves you and doesn't want to. Even if it's when she dies.*

*Monica, the way for you to heal this is to be held by the universal mother, to let go of this fear of abandonment, and feel the love and support that is always there for you and everyone, and for you to share this message: this love is always here.*

*The veil between the physical world and the spiritual world is very thin. You've known this ever since you were a child and felt the presence of the spirit of the man who died in your family home. This is your earliest memory of connecting with spirits and having the call to make the most of this precious life. Life is to be lived fully. Revel in your body. Don't deny it, enjoy it. Play. Experience your capacity for deep pleasure and joy in this body. Explore sacred sexuality, earthly love and divine connection. Know that this wisdom of making the most of being here needs also to be shared.*

*You can do this. You can help yourself and help others, enable them to get back into their truth. Know what you need to be. Trust your intuition, your guts, release your chains. Reclaim your "No" and honour your "Yes". It's time to take action.*

*Look after yourself first so you can give from overflow. Know there is absolute wisdom in this.*

*I want you to break through, clear the chains and cut them off. Step away from the ties that bind you. Be who you are and take right action. This is your turn. The time is yours now, Monica. Heal, recover, come back, and share all that it is you're here to share.*

*With love and boundless blessings from your biggest fan, lover and supporter.*

*Monica xxx*

**What golden nuggets did you learn from this experience?**

Our life experiences enable us to grow in power, strength and wisdom. The stories we have lived through can give us the courage to take action and realise our life purpose.

Behind all the experiences is an unbroken thread of loving support provided by the God of my understanding that I see as universal, infinite love. I am blessed to feel supported and loved by God, angels, guides and ancestors.

As one of my mentors, Easton Hamilton from The Reach Approach, says, the boat of truth may rock and pitch, but it will never sink. Trust that more.

Open your heart to be compassionate. Compassion can sometimes require you to say no. Firstly be compassionate with yourself, so you can then develop compassion for others.

It is our job to emancipate ourselves from the bonds that tie and bind us. We are at choice. We can ask for help and support but, ultimately, we are the ones who have to take off the chains and move once we realise we have been untethered.

The body always works in our best interests, even when it doesn't feel that way. Listen to the body more, she doesn't lie.

Make the most of the time you have with the people you love and care about; you never know when that time will run out.

Know that it is important for you to give yourself time and space to grieve for your losses and acknowledge the life changes.

Like the wooden doll, we recognise our wholeness when all of our versions are revealed, the stories are told, and we put ourselves back together. We are sovereign. We are whole. We are complete.

**What would you tell other women who might be experiencing this?**
When you receive a life challenge or loss, take time to consider what you need as a minimum in order to be well environmentally, physically, emotionally, mentally and spiritually.

Make sure you take action before you forget. Even small steps and writing down your wisdom and insight will help you to maintain momentum and learn the lessons life is here to teach you. Ask for and receive support, mentoring and guidance.

The power of forgiveness is phenomenal. Remember to forgive yourself for all the things you have done to yourself and to others. Forgive others for all they have done to you consciously or unconsciously.

**What are some of the things you would have changed in this situation if you could?**
I would have opened up more to the whisperings of my body, heart, mind and soul. I would have trusted the power and strength and wisdom of my body, womb and guts. I would have stopped doing things I know were out of alignment with my core values.

In reality though, I wasn't ready to change until the moment that I was ready. It has unfolded as it was meant to.

**Any final words?**

Open your heart and trust your gut; include the wisdom of your digestive system and your womb in your decision-making.

If in doubt, start with a clear-out. Begin with a simple declutter: this will create space for you to take stock of your environment and listen to the wisdom of your body, heart, mind and soul. Let universal love, God and Spirit show you the way and then take action.

**How can people get in touch with you?**

- LinkedIn, Facebook, Instagram, YouTube: **Monica Cor Auri**
- *www.monicacorauri.com*
- Business Wellbeing® Global: *www.businesswellbeingglobal.com*
- Spiritual Kitchen Podcast: *https://soundcloud.com/thespiritualkitchen*

"Do not hesitate to ask for support and help! You do not have to pretend to anyone including yourself, that you are made out of iron! You do not have to deal with your struggles alone! Seek support, seek help, just do it for yourself. You deserve it."

– Anna Kupisz-Cichosz –

# Little Bear

### Anna Kupisz-Cichosz

*Businesswoman, financial strategist, CEO of Softway LTD*

**W**hat are you passionate about and how are you contributing to the world?

My passion lies in taking tired and exhausted business owners from debt to millions. Over the last six years, I have consulted with and helped more than 3,000 entrepreneurs regain control over their money in their private and business lives so they could stop struggling financially and start fulfilling their missions and dreams about truly living.

I feel overjoyed when I see the women I work with achieving huge shifts in the way they perceive their business. It is so rewarding to see them recalculating their whole business, setting the right financial goals, adjusting prices and gaining the courage to stop limiting themselves and their vision.

My vision is to see hundreds of thousands of women fulfilling their mission and living the lifestyle they want to live instead of struggling financially. I want them to understand and experience that making money in their business is not about survival: it is about living, truly living.

**Describe a pivotal time in your life you wish to share.**
The pivotal moment that changed my life was the death of my father when I was seventeen years old. His death brought an awareness and insight into what it was like to struggle financially. The loss of my father caused us to face hardship as the remuneration of both my parents was needed to support our family, and it was my father who earned more at that time. However, for you to understand why that made such an impact on me, I need to take you back to the time I was born.

You need to know that back then Poland was a communist country and just ten days before I was born, 'martial law' was introduced in my country. Not only was the economic situation really bad, as the shelves in every shop were empty, but also the social unrest and dissatisfaction reached extremely high levels, as the government was afraid of losing control and power.

Imagine now my mum having me as an infant, struggling to buy soap, toilet paper, diapers or even milk to feed me. Imagine a system where you are only allowed to buy 1 kg of meat and one bar of soap per month, not because you don't have the money, but because you were not given tickets allowing you to buy more of these products.

I remember my mum and I doing shopping in a butcher's shop when I was five years old and asking my mum if we could buy some beef and ham as I saw it on the shelf, and I knew she had money in her wallet. But my mum smiled at me and said that unfortunately we did not have the ticket to buy it, but we could buy some pork and a little chocolate bar.

Then, when I was eight years old, I remember people really struggling financially because of the galloping inflation. As a result, you could sell your car one day and three days later you were only able to buy a bike for the same amount of money. Life was a struggle and all about standing for hours in queues to buy necessities; this was a normal part of our daily routine. Normal people just could not truly live and make their dreams come true, as the reality at that time was just to satisfy the basic needs with no problems.

Although the times changed when I was nine or ten years old when communism came to an end, those memories of struggling were still locked tightly within my genes!

**Looking back, what made it such an important part of your life journey?**
There is of course a reason why I wrote about these early memories. Looking back, I see now that I grew up seeing people have money but not being able to buy anything but the essential goods as there was none on the shelves in the stores. I also had friends whose parents decided to leave their children for a year with grandparents in order to go to the USA or Norway to work illegally to send their families money or buy goods they couldn't get at home.

At the same time, as a child, I felt life had something more to offer than just financial struggle, and with the change of the political system in Poland, my parents found a way to move themselves into a new situation where they did not have to struggle any more. So as a teenager I experienced a life where money was not a problem, where life was not about struggle but about making deep hidden dreams, like travelling around Europe, come true.

But the truth is the death of my father awoke all the emotions that were hidden under my memories from my early childhood and mobilised me into action, as I felt the struggle would begin again, but this time for me.

The death of my father forced me to overcome again, but this time on a conscious level, all the emotions and patterns I received as a child from my parents, grandparents and the whole society I lived in. It forced me to face again financial struggle and figure out how to cope. When I was younger, this involved developing skills that would allow me to run my business and generate money to support the family; as an adult, learning how to cope with the deepest financial panic when I saw that potential bankruptcy was just three months away. I learnt that you need to change the course of your actions in business and start implementing new financial habits.

All these experiences have made me the person I am today. They have allowed me to develop crucial skills in financial planning, financial goal setting and product pricing. My experience has also allowed me to share my experiences with my clients and help them emotionally get through the whole technical business process of finances with me by their side.

**Based on the wealth of knowledge, wisdom, and experience you have now, what would you have liked to say to yourself back then?**

*Dear Ann,*

*I am writing back to you at the sweet age of seventeen. I know at this time you feel so secure, loved and happy and with the fabulous holidays stretching ahead of you, you can relax and enjoy yourself, especially now you know your parents have reached a point in their lives where money is not a problem any more.*

*Just thinking of your parents brings such joy; you feel so blessed to have the bond you do with your father. Not every girl has the morning ritual of breakfast in bed brought to her by her father, but you do, and he loves to take you shopping too. He really does want the best for you, which is why he always takes you to the best shops where you can buy the finest clothes and shoes. Do you remember when a year ago he bought you two Barbie dolls? He laughed, that ten years ago when you were just a little girl, he couldn't buy them in Poland, as it was a semi-communist country and impossible to find them in the shops, but he wanted you to have them so badly, he decided to buy you two now. He does love to make you laugh.*

*I know you feel free and amazing while spending time with your father. Even when you were a little child, climbing trees in holey or dirty clothing was never an issue as he just wanted you to be joyful, happy and carefree. Which is probably why he never called you by your name, but instead by a nickname he gave you that meant "little bear that loves playing." Your dad just loves you the way you are. And now as a teenager, you know he is so proud of you, of your accomplishments, like you teaching small children English and German and earning money for little pleasures instead of asking your parents for pocket money. You know he takes great joy picking you up from the extra classes you love to have and talking about how your day was and laughing at your jokes.*

*I know that sometimes it can feel more emotionally difficult for you to deal with your mother, but it's really good you know and feel you can rely on her too. I want you to know that running the household in those first difficult years of your life, where it was hard to get toilet paper or even a bar of soap due to communism, may have made her feel like she had the weight of the world on her shoulders. I know you don't have such a strong bond with her like with your father, but you know that she works a lot, not only as a teacher at school but also giving private lessons at home. Thanks to those lessons, your parents will always be able to cope financially in difficult times. Maybe there were times they couldn't buy everything they wanted, but at least they could buy all the things that were needed. Those private lessons your mother taught also give you the money for all the additional classes or private lessons you want.*

*When I look at you now, I feel joy that you had the first seventeen years of your life carefree. But Ann, I need to tell you something, and this is not easy for me, but you need to know that this summer will be the most fabulous and the most horrible in your life. Things will happen that will change you and influence your whole life. You will experience the deepest sorrow and grief. You will experience the fear and anger. You will also feel sorry for yourself. But I want you to know you will figure it out, how to cope and gain strength from all these experiences. What is more, you will become inspirational for other people and you will help hundreds of women.*

*But let's start from the beginning. After a fabulous trip to Italy in July you'll visit your friend Kate in the south-west of Poland. You will have a great time there and will want to come back from that trip alone by train. However, your dad will not allow that to happen and, as you know how much he likes driving the car with you and having fun together, you will agree that both of your parents can pick you up from your friend. You love your dad so much you'll decide it is not worth arguing with him about it. Besides, next year when you turn eighteen, you will be able to travel alone, so you will decide that one year will not make a difference. But it did!*

*Unfortunately, your parents will never pick you up from your friend; twenty kilometres before they reach the town, they will be involved in a car accident. One of the damaged cars will be that of your parents and it is in that car, your dad will die. You won't know this until you get to the hospital. When you walk in through the doors, you will hear your father's friend talking to the ambulance crew about the accident. You will hear just part of the sentence, "didn't stand a chance", and at that moment you will know your father has died and your mother survived.*

*In this moment you will experience consciously for the first time how fast your analytical skills can work. How fast you are able to draw the right conclusions from bits and pieces of information. You may ask why it's important for me to write about this to you now? But I want you to know that fast, analytical thinking will be used often and will become very valuable throughout your life.*

*Thanks to that skill, you will realise within one second only your mother knew the address and telephone number of your father's friend, and only she could have let you know, with the help of hospital, there was an accident. So, hearing that part of the sentence, you will know it was your father who did not stand a chance. Being conscious your father is dead will enable you to pull yourself together and go to your mother. You know you are incapable of helping your father now, but you can still take care of your mother. You know she loves your father so much; he is the man of her life. You heard a hundred times the stories of their love, how it started, how quickly they decided they loved each other, getting engaged after only three months of knowing each other. So you know she will fall to pieces as she has lost the person she loved most.*

*When you finally find her, you barely recognise her. Ann, don't be afraid; it just looks bad, but she's fine, taking into account the shape of their car after the accident. It was a miracle she had only a few broken bones and light concussion. When you see her, she will utter a sentence that will change your life. First, you will hear from your mother it was not your fault; it was just an accident that could happen to anyone. But you already know that, however the second sentence that was spoken louder will have a graver consequence on your life. You will hear a statement that wasn't even directed to you. It was a question that your mother will ask herself: "How will we cope financially?" You've just experienced financial security for the first time and, only a few months ago, you've heard your parents say you have enough money to buy a new car, that you can afford your trip to Italy and they can afford your dream English course in the UK next year. And yet here you are again, with financial struggle, as you start all over.*

*You will feel the tension flowing from your mother and pure fear she will not manage to cope financially. At this moment you know what you will do! At this moment the carefree young and joyful girl that had lots of adventures, will vanish for many, many years. Unasked, you will take the heaviness of financial struggle on your shoulders. At this moment you will decide the allowance you will be given because of the death of your father from the state, you will give to your mother, and this will be one way you can contribute to the household. It will be something like one fifth of your father's remuneration, but still it is something. What is more, you know you will need to prepare yourself for final exams you have in ten months' time, your entrance exams for university, and also increase the numbers of kids in business teaching English and German lessons.*

*Ann, on the day your father died, the nickname he gave you will die too. It seems that after the death of your father, neither your brother nor your mother will have the courage to call you by the nickname your father gave you, as it brings up too many memories and painful emotions.*

*Ann, next year you will need to start developing a small foreign language school in your part of the city in order to grow your business and increase your income. You will learn how to gain clients, how to talk to them, persuade them, negotiate with them and, I want to tell you, you will succeed in all of it. Over the next four years you will spend time teaching children English and German, dealing with their parents and occasionally having time to have fun with your friends. You will become a very responsible person.*

*After four years, even your brother will tell you that you are a student and that you should be having fun, as this is supposed to be the best time of your life. You should party and try different things, but you won't, you will just study and work and your life will become boring. Your brother will be insistent and this will be one of the first wake-up calls. Ann, he won't back down: he will encourage you to take the tests needed to gain a scholarship to Germany and I want to tell you, you deserve to have the freedom to do this, you deserve to do something for you now, especially as your mother will get her finances under control. In fact, she will become an inspiration to you, as she gets her career back on track. She will be able to take care of you, but you will be in this repeating pattern of self-sacrifice that you can't just stop. But you have to. It is your time to become carefree again.*

*In Germany, you will rediscover your own dreams. In Germany, you will discover you have the power to bring them to life one by one. In Germany, you will rediscover YOU. You also learn one of the most valuable lessons, earning money is not about survival, it is about living, truly living.*

*Ann, even twenty years later you still will miss your father. You would love nothing better than to sit next to him on the couch, put your head on his shoulder like you used to do when you were a teenager and watch a good movie together. Unfortunately, the pain and sorrow will not disappear, but you will learn how to gain strength and sensibility from it. On the other hand, you will build and develop a special bond with your mother. It will not be easy, as you need to learn to accept each other, but I can tell you the reward is worth the effort. I know it might be difficult to believe now, but you will understand each other really well, and you will experience a deep and sincere relationship with her. You need to know that even now she is your greatest supporter and will help you whenever you need her.*

*You are really lucky and blessed; I want you to know that you will not struggle financially for a long time. Yes, you will experience financial struggles, you will even experience being nearly broke, but not only will you manage to overcome all the troubles, but this will be a precious experience that will support you in your work!*

*You will become a business owner, you will gain your financial freedom and security. And, what's most important, you will use your experience, knowledge, analytical business skills and your intuition to help other women in overcoming financial struggles, so they can find a balance and fulfil their life missions and start dreaming again. I know how surprising it may sound now, but you will become a financial strategist; you will teach others how to calculate their private and business budget, set financial goals and sales targets, calculate prices and manage finances. You will use your mentoring and coaching skills to empower people you work with, so they can implement all the financial plans and calculations, although many of them will be sure this is beyond their skills before they start working with you. But the most important thing will be you will teach others not only how to regain control over money, releasing the fear of not having it, but also teach them how to generate money to live the lifestyle they really want, make their dreams come true and gain self-fulfilment by accomplishing their life's mission.*

*Ann, a fabulous life is ahead of you, and I want you to know that.*

**What golden nuggets did you learn from this experience?**
First of all, I realised all our memories, those we are aware of as well as those hidden in our mind, shape us, create our life experience and make us a beautiful person. They also drive us or force us to acquire new skills so we can cope and manage to live life with quality and on our terms. The only thing we really need to do is to face them and all emotions they include. Do not try to run away from difficult or bad experiences, as eventually you will manage to gain strength from them and the magic will start to happen. You will be surprised at the beautiful things you will be able to give, not only to other people but, foremost, to yourself.

What is more, the death of my father taught me I do not have to understand everything good or bad that happens to me, but the first step is to work on all of the emotions and gain strength, belief and sensibility out of them, accepting them and embracing them. Life in denial, suppressing or neglecting emotions, rejecting your own weaknesses will only stop your own personal growth and even might impact destructively on your health and spirit. You are at your most beautiful with all the colours you have inside, you just need to let them shine.

**What would you tell other women who might be experiencing this?**
If you are experiencing difficult times now that are affecting your financial life, I want you to know that, as Steve Jobs once said, "You can't connect the dots looking forward; you can only connect them looking backwards." So, you have to trust that the dots will somehow connect in your future. You have to trust in something – your gut, destiny, life, karma, whatever. I feel that my dots are connecting and, although I have no idea what will happen in my life, I just KNOW my intuition will help me make the best choices so the dots will connect in the most beautiful and best way for me! I just need to listen carefully to my own voice and not be afraid of asking for help if I need it.

**What are some of the things you would have changed in this situation if you could?**
I remember that after the death of my father, I did not want to be a burden to anyone. Especially to my mum or my brother. I saw their pain and did not want to burden them with all I was feeling and what I was going through. I also didn't want my teachers and friends to worry about me, so for a long time I hid my feelings and emotions and did not turn to anyone for help. And I have paid my price for it. So, if you ask me if there are things I would have changed and I could have changed, it would be turning to a specialist for help, so I could accept and embrace these experiences earlier than I did.

**Any final words?**

Just one sentence: Do not hesitate to ask for support and help. You do not have to pretend to anyone, including yourself, you are made of iron! You do not have to deal with your struggles alone. Seek support, seek help, just do it for yourself. You deserve it!

**How can people get in touch with you?**

If you would like to get in touch with me, you can always find me on:
- Facebook: *@anna.kupisz.mentor*
- LinkedIn: *www.linkedin.com/in/annakupiszcichosz/*
- Website: *www.annakupisz.com*

"Treat yourself with compassion as you are human. Don't hate yourself for the thoughts and feelings you have for they are just stories. And if you made them up, you can make anything up. So, choose instead to live as the divine and beautiful spirit that you truly are."

– Joanna Harris –

# Your Stories Aren't Real

## Joanna Harris

*CEO and founder of The Oneness Movement and the myTOM platform, the home of conscious well-being. Strategic visionary and experienced change consultant in financial services. Cat lover, gin drinker.*

**W**hat are you passionate about and how are you contributing to the world?

I have studied conscious well-being for over ten years, and through my own life-long transformation journey, I have explored a myriad of disciplines and experiences to find my own oneness. I am passionate about helping people explore their own journey.

There is not a one-size-fits-all, and at different times, different people, concepts or experiences can help us feel whole, gain insights to our truth and feel connected. I am on a mission to bring oneness into our everyday lives. Energy is our true nature and it is time we all came home to our inherent connection. The world needs no more separation.

**Describe a pivotal time in your life you would like to share.**

At age thirty-one, I had a breakdown and checked myself in to a mental hospital. It was no great surprise to me I had ended up there, as I had hated myself for so long that it seemed inevitable. It was a desperate cry for help because the weight of my existence had grown so heavy, that I knew if I did not get help, I would lay down the burden forever.

**Looking back, what made it such an important part of your life journey?**

In the four weeks I stayed there, I found such a precious gift of not having to be me! All the beliefs I made up about who I was and all the feelings I felt about myself were not real. It was such a liberating experience – when nobody, not even you, expects anything of you, even sanity, you feel so completely free. I do laugh about this now as it was, seriously, one of the best times of my life. From there, I have gone on to learn so much about myself and how I created these self-hating beliefs. Now, I see them for what they are; simply made-up stories I don't need to believe in or live out anymore.

**Based on the wealth of knowledge, wisdom and experience you have now, what would you like to say to yourself back then?**

*Dear Joanna,*

*I am writing to you nearly a decade on from where you are now, aged thirty-one, and in a mental hospital, your life, once again, having fallen apart. I know you hurt so much right now and feel so completely alone, so desperate and so lost.*

I remember how much you cried that day you arrived. Sitting alone on the floor in the dark, tears streaming down your face and wailing loudly as the deep, self-torturing pain was released.

Although you don't know it now, this will be one of the best experiences of your life. You will surrender so completely to the pain, give up all control and allow yourself for the first time to be vulnerable and supported by others.

It is hard for you to see now, as you sit there crying and releasing your pain, but I promise you, this is the start of your healing. I know I can't change what has happened to you, but I want to take you back into your past to show you a different way to view your life, the way I see it now.

When you were thirteen, you were every parents' dream; a popular, highly intelligent child, bright and personable. You kept your room tidy, helped with housework, obeyed the rules and seemed to be good at everything you put your hand to. On the outside. On the inside, you felt dead.

You hated yourself so much. You felt there was something so fundamentally wrong with you and that you just didn't belong. You were also starting to realise that nobody really understood you because, if they did, they'd know the pain you were in. And you hated them, for their inability to see the real you.

But you see, these feelings of not belonging were not true, it was a made-up story already deeply ingrained in you. You didn't know *this though, and it felt so real to you, and so you played it out and started to create situations that would prove your story true.*

*You decided to test everyone to see if they really did want to know you. You became Gothic, with black and purple hair and even a half-melted Barbie doll stuck with pins hanging from your school bag. You thought if people truly liked you, they would look beyond the outside and see who you were on the inside.*

*I wish I could have told you back then you were just living out your story of not belonging, to prove your beliefs right. But you wouldn't have listened to me back then. You wouldn't have let anyone in, in case they really did see the truth you knew about yourself – you were fundamentally flawed and should not exist.*

*If I could have told you though, that this 'truth' about you was not true at all, things would not have gotten so bad. You were not and are not flawed and you really do deserve to exist. It was just that, in your early childhood, you felt unwanted, and made up your belief that it meant there was something wrong with you. We all get wounded in our childhood, and we have all made up our own beliefs about what this means about us. It becomes who we are and how we define our self—our personality, thoughts and feelings. You held on to this childhood story so tightly, it consumed your behaviour.*

*Now you know there was nothing terribly bad about your childhood and your parents; no abuse, no violence or drugs. Your parents were a typical couple married in the early seventies. They were raised by their own parents during the fifties and sixties, in a time when "children should be seen and not heard," so, ok they were not the best communicators.*

*Your mum suffered post-natal depression for six months after you were born. When you were two, her thyroid played up, making her feel crazy and have sleepless nights for many months. Her husband was barely aware anything had been wrong. Feelings just weren't spoken about.*

*Your father provided for the family. In his upbringing though, women were kind of second-class – and they had had three daughters (you being the youngest). While he did always want a son, he was not neglectful to his girls. It was just that he only really showed you affection in public, where other people could judge him as being a wonderful father. He would also often criticise your mother's suggestions or opinions, mostly because they came from a woman.*

*Their marriage broke down when you were about four, following an explosive argument. After the years of put-downs and witnessing the hypocrisy of him being a loving father in public but disregarding his children in private, the tension became too much for your mum. They argued bitterly and he moved out that night. When six weeks of counselling amounted to nothing, they agreed to go their separate ways.*

*Your parents were just people, doing the best they could. I know you understand this now, rationally. But to the infant that you* were then, when you were just looking for love and validation, this was traumatic! You felt a separation from your mother through her post-natal depression, and you felt neglect from your father, who was never there to show you how you were supposed to be in the world.

This is where you made up beliefs about yourself to make sense of why you didn't get love when you wanted it. You made up that there must be something wrong with you which meant you were unlovable, that you didn't belong and shouldn't exist.

As an infant, when our whole world consists of two people, our mum and dad, the situations we experience are real. But the meaning we apply to them should stay in the past with them, and not be applied to all people, in all situations, forever. Yet we take our childish beliefs and our self-definition and carry them into our adult lives – and then we make decisions and live out our personalities based on the beliefs of a two-year-old!

Luckily, you also made up some positive beliefs. Your mother was a strong woman, and she chose her daughters over her marriage. She knew you deserved move than just a public parade of love. She has been a tower of strength throughout your life. You believe women are strong and that you have your own inner strength. I can tell you this belief, from her, is why you kept fighting to survive, despite all the dark days, and why you chose to get help.

Your twenties were another journey of creating situations to prove to yourself you didn't belong. Under the guise of seeing the *world, you left your family (and some acquaintances, as you didn't really allow yourself to have real friends) to go off travelling. You thought that, out there in the world, you would find yourself and life may start to make sense. Surely there was somewhere in the world where you would belong? What seemed on the surface to be a marvellous experience, was just running away from everyone you believed didn't love you, including your family.*

*You didn't care for your sisters and cousins, so why would they care if you were gone? After all, you had grown up with them telling you that you did not exist because you did not have a birth certificate. They would pair off together and leave you out of their games, except for their favourite game of seeing who could make you cry each day.*

*Children can be cruel, that is true. But the pain you felt from their taunts was because you already believed yourself that what they said was true. There is a little saying that you cannot upset a dog by teasing it about not being able to fly. Flying does not matter to a dog. As people, we only hurt in relation to the things we believe. And you believed you were not wanted.*

*In your travels though, you did go on to find people that wanted you. Men. Sometimes just for a night. And you did find a way to connect with others, but only temporarily until the drugs wore off. And in both cases, the inevitable comedown and self-loathing would follow. I could write for hours on all the situations you created while away travelling, but really, they are all the same. You were lost, you were far away from home, you were alone, and you hated yourself. You kept looking for some connection, something to give you a sense of belonging in the world, something to make you feel that you did exist. But they were fake attachments and deep down you knew it, and you hated yourself more for it.*

*What I wish I could have shown you then was that you were just creating more situations to prove to yourself you didn't belong. You were living your same belief pattern, just in different towns, with different people playing parts in your story. Granted, the stories did have moments of pleasure, definitely! But these were short-lived, and you used them to hide from your feelings of not belonging. You could run away from home, but you couldn't run away from yourself.*

*In your late twenties, after you created a failed marriage where your husband left you for another woman, a failed attempt to live back home in Australia and be part of your family, and several failed attempts at holding down a job and creating a group of friends, you decided enough was enough. It was time to fix yourself. Now you had evidence from your past about what was wrong with you. You were a slutty, drug addict who treated others atrociously and did not make use of the brains you were given.*

*So, with that inner strength of yours, you set about solving this problem and fixing your fundamental flaws so people would like you and you would belong! You studied hard at accountancy and passed your exams. You got a job with a financial data company and made friends with colleagues. You were given many opportunities at work; your boss liked you and you were promoted. You had a few relationships, and a lovely house-share with great housemates.*

*Life was finally on the up. You suppressed the feelings of self-loathing and really tried hard to connect with people, even though this still scared you and gave you anxiety. You even had a best friend for the first time. And then you met the man of your dreams and would start a relationship, that would lead you to where you are now: alone, desperate and ready to die.*

*He was everything you thought you should have been. An Oxford graduate lawyer working for a top law firm in the City and on his way to partnership. A national table tennis champion, an artist, a pianist. He was from a loving family, posh, rich and well-connected. He would take you on holidays and dining in all the top restaurants and buy you nice things.*

*For two years, you lived in a happy dream, somewhat arrogantly though, because you had finally "made it". You had turned your life around and fixed yourself. You lived in a wonderful new house, in a trendy neighbourhood with everything you wanted, and you became an insufferable, stuck-up snob. You were trying so hard to be someone, and once again, you inevitably created a situation where you didn't belong and no one would love you. And the pain came when you realised you were not really fixed, and it was all an illusion, another stage for your belief story.*

*On a night seemingly like any other, two years into your marvellous relationship, your partner came home from work and matter-of-factly stated he didn't love you and was leaving. You were stunned, having thought this would end with a fairy tale wedding and a happily-ever-after. Although it was his house, he packed some things and left you that night. You sat there alone, in shock and crying on the kitchen floor with a knife at your throat and a trickle of blood running down your neck.*

*How you made it through that night, I don't know. I always put it down to that inner strength from your mum. It certainly was not because of your best friend, who refused to come over to support you, thinking you were completely over-reacting.*

*The next couple of weeks were a blur as you tried to pull yourself together. After all, you were on familiar ground of life falling apart. You knew the drill. You're alone, you can't rely on anyone else, no one will help you, no one loves you, so smile on the outside and die on the inside.*

*You moved out, finished your exams, found a new job starting in a few months, saw the doctor to go back on the antidepressants, put on a brave show to your friends, and even managed a trip back home to see your family. I think you even believed yourself you were fine as you had sorted out the mess of your life, again.*

*And then one day, on the way to work, you stopped at the doctors to collect your prescription and, while in his office, you broke down and finally asked for help. And this is where you are now, Joanna, and, believe me, despite the pain you are going through, this really is the best thing that will happen to you.*

*Allowing yourself to be vulnerable, to open up and share and to be held by others during your darkest time, will be a cleansing and cathartic process. It will hurt as you release all the pain and sorrow from having hated yourself for so long, but in letting it out, you find release and freedom from having to live out the beliefs of your infant self.*

*Joanna, let me now tell you the wonderful life you create after this experience. You develop an incredible relationship with your family. You and your mum will become closer than ever and will travel the world together. You will be friends with your sisters, whose children will love you as their loving aunty. You will make peace with your dad before he passes away and have welcoming arms for his wife, your stepmum.*

*You will excel in your career as a management consultant in financial services and it will give you financial stability and a beautiful house of your own. You will have two darling cats, whom you love and adore so completely.*

*You will have a beautiful, loving and deeply passionate relationship of nine years (and counting) with a man who knows you truly, warts and all, and loves you incredibly for your true self. You will have an amazing group of friends, a coach and a community who also see you just as you are, your brilliance and your egoic stories, and they will love you and help keep you on your true path.*

*And the best part of all, Joanna; you will no longer try to fix yourself. You will understand these stories, how you created them and why you lived them out. You will understand they are a part of you and will always be, but they don't have to define who you are and what you want to create going forward. You will see that you have a choice, to live those stories over and over, or to create what you love. And that is what you choose!*

*You will create an amazing business, The Oneness Movement, whose vision is to bring connection with ourselves, with others and with the universe, into our everyday lives. You will work with an amazing team to bring this vision into reality. Your business launches a platform which enables practitioners from holistic and well-being disciplines, who support others on their transformational journeys, to connect with their audiences, and you provide those audiences with resources and tools to support their journey.*

*You will be passionate and dedicated in helping other people find their connection, and embrace their true nature, so they can find peace and happiness in their own, fulfilling lives. Your journey will be rewarding and continue to enrich your life. It will not always be plain sailing, but you will keep choosing not to live back in your story, but instead to create a life you truly love.*

*Love and compassion always,*

*Joanna*

**What golden nuggets did you learn from this experience?**
Life is created from the stories we made up in childhood. But it doesn't have to be that way. We have a choice. We generally accept there is an energy which is the essence of everything in the universe,

including ourselves. We are all from that energy and by coming into human form, we can have an individual experience, through our own body, mind, and soul. Our energy comes into this vehicle in which to experience the world, and so it seeks to work out how it is here.

As a child, we seek validation from our parents to understand ourselves as individuals. From our mother, we want nurture and to know we are loved, and from our father we want to understand our place in the world. As they are only humans themselves, invariably at some stage, our validation will not be met. This hurts, so we try to make sense of why we hurt.

Understanding this 'why' then creates our definitions about our self, others and the world. And these definitions become the lens through which we then see everything. We then focus on avoiding the pain of unmet validation, guided by these definitions. But our focus creates our reality and what we resist will persist, because by focusing on not having that pain, we are actually still focusing on that pain.

Hence, we unconsciously create life situations which reinforce our beliefs. The more it happens, the more adamantly we believe it and we collect a life full of evidence to prove it! This is what being human is. We all do it. For some they believe they are not safe, or not good enough, others that they are powerless, or not capable, or not worthy. And then we go about our lives, trying to avoid the pain but keep recreating it.

The challenging part is that we truly believe it, because we think and feel it! But it's not reality, it's our lens of definition. Thoughts and feelings are in our mind, but our mind is nothing more than a culmination of everything we have thought and felt before, starting with the first beliefs of our unmet validation.

Sounds gloomy, but it's actually liberating, as it means that all things we tell our self are not real. We made them up! They don't mean anything about who we really are. And who we really are, is divine. Our true nature is the pure energy from which we are created. So, once you can see your stories, and recognise them as just that, you no longer have to live them, and you can choose to live as divine.

**What would you tell other women who might be experiencing this?**
Do not beat yourself up for the story that you may be living, however painful the circumstance and however traumatic the situation, it doesn't mean anything about you. It's structural, not personal. You are divine. Your true nature is pure, creative energy; you are the light and you can live as the sovereign queen of your own life. All you need to do is choose it.

If what I have said resonates with you, and you can start to look back on your life and see these patterns from your own story playing out, then welcome to the rest of your life! This is the first step to freeing yourself from beliefs that don't serve you. All you need to do is notice them, not fix them. Just have awareness, as the more aware you become, the more you will start to see them before they play out, so you can then choose something different.

And maybe you can't see your own patterns just yet; don't worry either. Luckily, conflict is a great tool for self-awareness! As I said about the dog not being able to fly, we only hurt in relation to the things we believe. Start by noticing what triggers you when you are in conflict, that charge you feel, that thing that winds you up, is an indication that you have a belief about yourself, others and the world. So simply ask yourself what definitions you are holding about yourself, others and the world, whenever you experience conflict, and that will start to show you your beliefs.

**What are some of the things you would have changed about that situation if you could?**

Not one tiny thing. If I had to go through all of this 100 times over to have the insight I now have about myself, so I can choose to create the life I want and not have to live that story, I would do it again and again. It is never too late, or too early, to recognise that you are divine, and be free from the story of your own personality, so you can live as your true and sovereign self.

**Any final words?**

Treat yourself with compassion, as you are human. Don't hate yourself for the thoughts and feelings you have, for they are just stories. And if you made them up, you can make anything up. So, choose instead to live as the divine and beautiful spirit you truly are.

**How can people get in touch with you?**

- Website: *www.theonenessmovement.com*
- Email: *Joanna.harris@theonenessmovement.com*
- Facebook: *www.facebook.com/theonenessmovement.com*
- Instagram: *@theonenessmovement*
- Twitter: *@onenessmovement*
- LinkedIn: *www.linkedin.com/company/theonenessmovement*

"Most of our greatest learnings come from tough times and experiences. They are there to show us how to grow and move forward and learn. If we are of an open mindset, we can see the world in a different way, which can be incredibly miraculous."

– Jo Tocher –

# Life After Baby Loss

## Jo Tocher

*Well-being and energy alignment mentor and coach*

**W**hat are you passionate about and how are you contributing to the world?

My mission is to work with women who have lost babies in pregnancy and guide them through the maze of emotions, so they can feel calm, centred, with clarity and direction for their future. I do this by helping them to tap into their mind, body, soul and energy, allowing them to live life on purpose and tap into their true purpose on this planet.

**Describe a pivotal time in your life you wish to share:**

I was working in Corporate Land, when I fell pregnant. This was unexpected, as my partner and I weren't planning children as we had just become engaged. It was unusual to fall pregnant, as I remember I was on my period and I felt it was safe (we used the rhythm method of contraception) but, this time, an embryo formed. Even more unusual was that it was a very determined male sperm! Once we talked about it, we were happy to be pregnant, but at twenty-three weeks our baby boy stopped developing, and he passed.

Understandably, this shocked us and shook me up, and I had a 360-degree turnaround. Life would never be the same. Corporate life wasn't for me any more and I felt driven to do something worthwhile with my life. Who knew then that I would train as a holistic therapist and work with women who were pregnant? I was halfway to living on purpose, and there was a part of me I didn't or couldn't face. Eventually, the universe put me on the right path, and I had a light bulb moment where I realised I could help other women who had lost babies! I had the first-hand experience of loss, and a tonne of holistic therapies under my belt. If I hadn't had my experience, I wouldn't be able to relate to women going through similar circumstances, help them, and guide them through the journey they're on now.

**Looking back, what made it such an important part of your life journey?**
If I hadn't experienced my baby loss, I wouldn't be on the path I'm on. I see it now as a gift. My baby loved me, and I loved him and carrying him for his short life span of twenty-three weeks in utero. It made me realise how much I wanted to have children, and I was lucky enough to then go on to have two beautiful girls. If I hadn't had my loss, more than likely I wouldn't have had my youngest daughter, because I didn't want more than two children. She came into my life for a reason; she teaches me every day how I can be better – a better parent and a better person. She is blessed with incredible emotional intelligence beyond her years.

Another gift my loss gave was the gift of living on purpose. By teaching and guiding others through the myriad of baby loss, I feel my life has purpose. How blessed I am to work in this field, fulfilling my purpose every day and leaving a legacy to help others, through my work and writing.

**Based on the wealth of knowledge, wisdom, and experience you have now, what would you like to say to yourself back then?**

*Dearest Jo,*

*I know how excited you are at this moment. You're waiting to go in and have your twenty-week scan and get the results of your amniocentesis. Although the scan is three weeks later than usual, you are not concerned.*

*When your partner suggests he would like to come along to be there as your support, you will tell him it's okay for you to do this alone; you'll leave work at lunchtime and go straight to the hospital. A simple, quick appointment, as you both saw the baby three weeks ago and made the decision not to find out the sex.*

*So, here you are again in the waiting room, ready to go in. In a minute you are going to be called in by the nurse, to give you the results of the amnio; you can stop holding your breath now, all will be good and clear. However, I do need you to brace yourself, as there will be news you don't expect on the scan. Don't worry, I'm right here with you, holding your hand ...*

*As they apply the gel to your stomach, you will look in anticipation at the screen. Pregnant women never grow tired of seeing the new life growing within; it's always so reassuring to hear the resonance of the heartbeat.*

*However, this day, even through the noise of the heartbeat, the room will suddenly go quiet, a stillness filling the air as you see the concentration on the sonographer's face change, as she turns the screen away from you, staring at it intently. Somehow, you will know something is amiss, but you will quietly tell yourself it must be okay, that you heard the heartbeat, everything is all right, surely, and this will become your mantra. You will ask if everything is okay as she rushes out the room, and she will reply she just has to double-check something and will be back with someone to take a look.*

*Left on your own, lying there, intuitively you will know, dear Jo, something isn't right, and, you will start to pray. As you lie there on the table feeling alone, I want you to know that you are never alone; I'm here with you and holding your hand, reassuring you that whatever happens, in the long run it will be okay. I know: I've seen life on the other side of this experience.*

*Finally, when she returns, she is joined by the consultant, who will briefly take a look, before turning to tell you there is an abnormality with your baby. There is fluid in his stomach and not enough in the amniotic sac. At that moment, she will turn the screen toward you, and what she shows you is something you'll never forget: your beautiful baby, with a distended stomach. I know right now how heartbroken you will feel, so lost, alone and confused.*

*As your mind frantically tries to process how this is even possible, the consultant will quietly ask you to dress and wait for her in the waiting room. As you sit there in the room, filled with all the other pregnant women, you won't be able to look at them, their faces full of hope and joy, when you're feeling dread, insecurity and incomprehension this could be happening to you.*

*Eventually, you will be called into the room to speak with the consultant. Although kind, she will tell you it's most likely your baby will not survive the pregnancy. At twenty-three weeks pregnant, this is a huge blow. How is this even happening? You made all the plans for how life was going to be when the baby was born, had the excitement at taking time off from your corporate job to be a mum. After all, at thirty-five, you are feeling ready to start a family.*

*You are sitting there trying to get your head around everything that has been said, not only because your beautiful, longed-for baby is unlikely to live, but also because your future has been thrown into the air. The consultant will ask you to make an appointment for you and your partner to come back the following day to discuss this further.*

*Leaving the consultant, you will just want to get home, back to the safety of your flat so you can cry and scream and process what has happened. Driving back, you will be in a state of shock, holding yourself together, while a thousand thoughts whirl.*

*When you get home, you won't be able to rest; you'll be on edge, trying to make the telephone calls to everyone who needs to know. The hardest call will be to your partner. As you explain not all is well, you will hear his voice down the phone trying to make sense of it all; he can't comprehend this either, and will rush home. When he walks through the door, you will see the look of shock on his face: why has this happened? He immediately blames the amniocentesis.*

*Calling work, you will tell them something is wrong, and you don't know when you'll be back.*

*The following day, you and your partner will return to the hospital, scared. You will wait, in the same waiting room with the other pregnant women, knowing your baby isn't okay.*

*When you are ushered into the room, the consultant will tell you that you have to make a choice – your baby isn't going to survive; you need to decide whether to have a termination or let nature take its course. This is not a choice a mum should have to make.*

*You will utter the words: "We will come back on Monday, when we have had time to consider all our options."*

*You will go home in a dazed and teary state. On a conscious level, you will both know it's the end of the road, but will keep the faith that maybe your baby will make a miraculous recovery – that hope is what will keep you going throughout the weekend. However, at one point during the weekend, you will feel a tearing pain in your belly.*

*On Monday, you and your husband will return to hospital, where you have the final scan and are told the worst news ever: your baby has died.*

*As you sit there in that room, a room normally filled with joy and happiness, you burst into tears; it's the worst moment of your life so far. Your partner will hold you and support you as he too tries to come to terms with your news. They will then ask you to come back to the hospital, to the labour ward, and deliver your baby at the end of the week.*

*You're so scared, you go into shutdown mode, trying to get through this. You will start to feel numb, like you're going through the motions of someone else's life. Jo, through this dark cloud, I want you to know that even though you cannot see it now, as the pain is too raw and painful, your view on this will change.*

*Eventually, delivery day will come. You and your partner will be in shock and numb, but your dear friend Judy, who is a trained nurse, will come too, able to ask the questions you both cannot form. This will be one of the toughest days of your life, but you are resilient and get through it.*

*You will be given pessaries to start your labour, and when the pain gets too much they will allow you to take morphine. Surprisingly, it won't seem to help much; your physical and emotional pain will be intense, as your body resists letting your baby go. However, Jo, you are more resilient than you know, and you dig deep to get through.*

*Your little boy (who you will call John, after your father) will be birthed eventually. When they ask you if you want to hold him, you will reply that if you did, you'd never be able to let him go. So instead they will wrap him in a blanket and put him on your chest so you can gaze at him, a baby, the size of your hand. Jo, this will be one of the saddest moments of your life, as you fight to comprehend why this has happened. It's a pivotal moment for you. John was there to put you on the right track, so you can follow your mission and help women around the world. However, you don't understand this for many years to come.*

*Eventually, they will ask you if you're ready to take him away. Jo, I know you will never be ready to let him go, but as they remove him from your chest, they take photos of him, and finger and handprints, and give him to your partner.*

*With empty arms, you're left on the bed with forceps on, as the placenta hasn't come out yet. After 45 minutes, your friend Judy will go to find the midwife, who has been called to an emergency, so you are left to process this with your partner and friend.*

*That night, you are taken to the ward. It's a maternity ward filled with women and their beautiful babies, which adds to the pain and emptiness inside; luckily, they will put you in a side room on your own. The night shift nurse, a beautiful, softly spoken Caribbean woman, will be the first person to say "I'm sorry for your loss." Although you will hear this often, it will be in this moment you are able to finally cry and cry and cry, silently into your pillow.*

*The next day, your partner will come to collect you, after you are given the all-clear to go home. Going home with empty arms will be very difficult; the whole world will look different and you will feel different. Your partner will stop at a shop and buy you croissants because he knows how much you like them, but you won't be able to eat; all you want to do is crawl into bed and scream and howl, like a primal woman, and be alone.*

*After a few hours you will feel the need to get up and go to the kitchen and do something, anything, just to bring normality back to your life, so you clean the whole kitchen, scrubbing the floor on your hands and knees, to release some of the energy.*

*Jo, my lovely, as if the trauma of giving birth is not enough, your body will take another beating. You will find yourself back in hospital, this time in A & E with a fever, admitted to the ward and put on an antibiotic drip for five days, with an infection, most likely caused by the long wait with the forceps on.*

*The time in hospital will give you time to truly process. You will be visited by the hospital counsellor, asked lots of questions you really didn't want to talk about yet, as it was too raw, too soon. Jo, it's okay for you not to answer the questions if you don't want to.*

*The hospital chaplain will also visit, asking if you want to have a service for John. I understand, Jo, that the thought of this sounds ways too morbid, but you will be grateful he insists, as the funeral will be lovely, intimate and very sad. Seeing that little coffin will be the saddest thing ever. However, that process will help to close a chapter for you both, and allow you to heal in your own way.*

*Before returning to work, you will fly home to NZ to be with your parents – it will be incredibly cathartic being at home with them, caring for you and allowing you to grieve.*

*Jo, returning to work approximately one month later will be hard, oh so hard. You will feel exposed, and that everyone is looking at you, but people don't know what to say, or how to behave. It will be a telling time, with you surprised by some people's actions, and horrified by others. You will expect the director of your department, a woman who also had many miscarriages, to be more caring and considerate, but instead she will expect you to just get on with it.*

*Jo, it's okay to need more time off, but it's not okay you weren't given the time you needed. Some bright spark in Corporate Land will decide they can't do without you and will believe that cognitive behavioural therapy is the answer, but not for you. This will be something you don't enjoy. The counsellor will be a French woman with very little empathy. Luckily for you, with CBT, there is always an end date, and you will become really good at faking being "just fine" until you compete the course and are released, somehow in their mind 'fixed'.*

*But you are not fine or fixed; how can you be? But don't worry, Jo, the universe has a way of working things out. One day at work, the chief exec will come and give your department a talk.*

*Speaking about his vision for the company, he will expect you and your colleagues to work hard to achieve.*

*This moment will bring clarity, it will be like a light bulb moment as you realise this is NOT your vision. You won't know what your vision is at the time, but you know that this is not it. You have changed so deeply; you realised corporate life was not for you any more. There must be more out there in the world than that, even if you didn't know what.*

*So you went on a mission, and the universe supported you with a magazine article, telling the story of a woman who had left corporate, because she was disenchanted with it, and followed her heart. The article will give you goosebumps, as you KNOW you need to do the same. She had trained as an aromatherapist, and you loved the sound of it, so you booked a taster weekend, eventually signing up to do a full-time diploma at the Tisserand Institute.*

*This will start you on your holistic and healing journey, discovering energy work, self-development and so much more. You will start to feel happy again, and reach a point three years later when you feel ready to try again for another baby. That little soul will be ready and waiting for you, and she will be the BEST thing that will happen in a very long time. You will find yourself, as becoming a mother to a beautiful baby girl was the missing piece of the puzzle for you. But then you wanted another one!*

*You got pregnant again, but you miscarried at eight weeks. By that time in your journey, you become very philosophical about it, because you knew it wasn't forming correctly and it wasn't the right time for you.*

*When you healed, you tried again, and were gifted another soul, another little baby girl blessing your life. And so begins a new journey; a new chapter of raising your two girls and working part-time in therapy work.*

*It will be when your beautiful girls are in high school that you will train in the Energy Alignment Method as a mentor, and during this process you will realise you are in a place where you can help other women who have gone through a similar experience to you. You can share the gift of experience to help other women get through these dark times too.*

*So, my darling girl, everything you went through was leading you to this point. The universe had it all mapped out, and you've learnt from your experiences that things do happen for a reason, even if it might take many years to understand. For you, it is your purpose to help other women. You had an almighty kick up the backside from the universe to get you on the right track, releasing Corporate Land to make way for the bigger picture unfolding.*

**What golden nuggets did you learn from this experience?**
Things happen in mysterious ways. When you go through a traumatic time in your life, you somehow find resilience to carry

on. Human beings are incredible – we have so much strength and resilience at times when we face adversity. It starts during our birth: if we can enter the world through the birth canal, which can be a turbulent experience, into a bright, noisy, scary world, we can get through most things in life.

I learnt that out of the darkness, the most incredible things happen.

People surprise you in ways you couldn't imagine – sometimes they are wonderful, and sometimes hurtful when they're not there for you. I feel this is a way of the universe showing us their true colours. Most of our greatest learnings come from tough times. They are there to show us how to grow, move forward and learn. If we are of an open mindset, we can see the world in a different way, which can be miraculous. However, if we are trapped in our problems and can only see them, we will stay there or spiral downwards. It is a choice of how we respond. We can view our life and lessons with interest and curiosity, or we can see them as gloom and doom.

The choice is ours – there are gifts everywhere, when we are ready to look for them, notice and find them. Know that the greatest gifts you receive come from the darkest times, and often we only realise this in hindsight. Quite often, things are right at the end of our nose, but we can't see them. Many times, it has taken someone I've worked with, a coach or mentor, to point it out to me. When we are guided to reach out to work with someone, or speak to someone, there is mostly a message there for us. Take heart, you had a pivotal moment in your life for a reason. Seek the answer, dig deep, it is there within you. It will define you and move you in the direction you're 'meant' to be going.

**What would you tell other women who might be experiencing this in their lives?**

Beautiful women, if you have lost a baby during pregnancy, you will find this incredibly hard to bear. My heart goes out to you. Just know that you are stronger than you think and braver than you know, and you will endure. In time, and it does take time, you will get through it. Know that, if you lock it away, it will come back to bite you in different ways. You will never forget, but you will come to a time when you can live with it, without it being constantly in your head. I found journaling and expressing my feelings beneficial. Do speak to your friends and family about how you feel, for they cannot understand, and often expect you to "get over it" quickly. It is difficult for them too, as they don't know what to say to you. Although people are sympathetic in the beginning, they will begin to forget your pain. You never will, so I advise you to find a community of people with similar experiences to yours to talk and reach out to. Find an empathetic ear, someone who has walked your journey. I spent time in counselling and therapy, with the wrong people who didn't have my experience. It left me feeling lonelier than ever. Do seek help, reach out, and if you haven't found the right person, keep looking. There will be someone for you. Please don't keep it locked away inside you – it will corrode you from the inside out. No matter if you've experienced a loss recently or years ago – it's never too late to seek help.

**What are some of the things you would have changed in this situation if you could?**

After much soul-searching, I wouldn't change a thing, because it led me to see everything I experienced; before, during and after was just as it was meant to be. Looking back now, I can see how my life unfolded perfectly. If there was one thing I could have changed, it would be the time it took for me to understand why it happened and to learn what my purpose in life is. However, that can't be changed and I'm philosophical that it unfolded in that way for a reason. Only, I would have loved to have helped more women going through their baby-loss journey.

**Any final words?**

If you have experienced a similar loss, please do not blame yourself in any way – blame is destructive. The biggest gift you can give yourself is love and compassion. You are worthy of both.

**How can people get in touch with you?**

- Email: *jo@light-after-loss.com*
- Website: *www.light-after-loss.com*

Read one of the *Life After Loss* series of books – *Life After Miscarriage – Your Guide to Healing from Pregnancy Loss,* available on my website and on Amazon.co.uk.

"We all have choices sometimes it is not the easy route that is the best choice, but trust whatever you face you will come through stronger – if you want to! Everything will be fine in the end."

– Caroline Purvey –

# Breaking the Chains of Our Past to Set Our Children Free

### Caroline Purvey

*CEO of TRE UK® and creator of the Total Release Experience®*

**W**hat are you passionate about and how are you contributing to the world?

My passion is to continue to inspire and empower the thousands of women globally who struggle day to day with stress, coping with the impact of trauma or have given up hope. I teach them how simple it is to take back control of their physical, mental and emotional well-being in the most powerful yet natural, innate way. We can all heal from our past, build resilience and teach our children to do the same. It is truly transformational work, giving hope where there isn't any.

I am so inspired by the courage of women who recognise that they alone hold the power to discover their true self, as they go through their self-healing journey and transform themselves to live the life they want.

**Describe a pivotal time in your life you wish to share.**
I have had many pivotal moments, but the one I choose to share is the one that had a most profound impact on me at the time and still resonates with me years later.

I am a great believer in synchronicity – things always happen for a reason. Sometimes we might not understand when something extraordinary happens, but it reveals itself when the time is right. I reflect back to 1981. With my husband, we visited John, a business supplier. He was in his last days as cancer took hold. I did not know him that well, but he was a lovely man. I sat on the edge of the couch where he lay and held his hand. As always, it was difficult to know what to say in such circumstances. I did say I was sorry he was suffering, and I thanked him for all the good work he had done. He squeezed my hand, looked at me in the eye and said: "You are going to do great work one day and achieve something quite amazing." I looked at him, taken aback I felt goose bumps – I did not really know what to say. Where did that come from? Was it a spiritual realisation that a dying man could see?

Seven years ago, my daughter was living in South Africa, and I assured her I would be there for the birth of her first baby. One night, one of my Yoga students told me about a training in South Africa, a practice for trauma release that I had never heard of. I decided to make a phone call that night to South Africa and find out more. It was unimaginable that five weeks later, I found myself in South Africa. I arrived on Monday, baby James was born on Wednesday and Friday, there I was, ready to train with ninety-nine other people from around the world in a venue I actually knew. It was only five minutes away from where my daughter lived! How did that all come together? Serendipity indeed.

I always say be careful what you wish for. I declared to all at the end of three days: *"I am going back to make this happen in the UK."* I had a vision and a mission. I returned and set up TRE UK® at the same time I opened my yoga studio. For the first time, I felt I was dealing with something that was going to be more powerful than anything I had ever learnt or experienced to help others heal. This work had found me, and now I understand why. Two years ago, I had a major breakthrough, when my work was accepted into a prison for male offenders. A vision I had long held. I thought of John's words. Wow, he was right. I never imagined all those years ago my life path and all my experiences would lead me to where I am now, and there is nowhere I would rather be.

**Based on the wealth of knowledge, wisdom and experience you have now, what would you like to say to yourself back then?**

*Dearest Caroline,*

*Welcome to the world. You don't know it yet, but you are destined for something special. But, like it or not, little one, the journey is not going to be easy. You are going to meet some bumps on the road. But you will grow strong and wise. You will be blessed with a heart full of love and compassion. Although your heart and trust will be broken many times, you will be strengthened by your challenges. That strength will bring you out to shine your diamond. Your destiny will set you on a path with a powerful global message: "We need to break the chains of our past to set our children free."*

*You are just three years of age and you are already at school; a little, private convent school in Eltham. You started very young, but back in 1955, that's how it was. One sunny Friday afternoon, you and your class will be told about a race. With your shoes, blazer, hat and satchel laid out along the tennis court, on the whistle, the first to run down the line and get dressed can go home early with Mummy and Daddy. Wow, you will be supercharged that day. You love your mummy and daddy so much you will give it your all. Your little legs will run like the wind, for you really wanted to be at home with them. Winning will be your goal, and you will succeed.*

*You will learn as a child that you made Mummy and Daddy proud because you made a real effort.*

*You will come to realise if you want something, go for it, and that love is your driving force. You will become a speed walker from that day on!*

*You are now eight and in the singing class, which you enjoy, but something will change that day. You and the rest of your class will be stood around the piano, wondering what you will sing next. You are all asked to sing a few bars individually. It is your turn and nervously you sing. But, in that moment, your self-esteem will be shattered as your singing teacher will tell you in front of the class you cannot sing, suggesting you are tone deaf! You will have a feeling of shame and despondency that you are the one without the voice. You will know in that embarrassing moment you will never again sing, for you will be telling yourself you can't. You will learn as a child you don't have a voice. Words can hurt.*

*You will come to realise the words of that one teacher impacted you for most of your life, an unintentional, thoughtless, throwaway comment. Being singled out in front of others made you feel worse. Words are powerful and, once said, cannot be erased.*

*Something will be suppressed in you that day, and there will be many times you will want to speak out in your life, to share how you feel, but something inside will stop you from sharing your true thoughts and feelings, even in your marriage. It will hit home when you are thirty-nine and at university. One of your tutors will say to you when he returns an assignment: "If only I could get into that head of yours; there is so much I would love to hear that you keep inside."*

*You will come to realise your voice had been suppressed for many years from the thoughtless, hurtful comments of adults. Words are powerful and, once said, cannot be erased.*

*At nine years of age, you and your eldest sister will be excited, as you will travel to your nan and pops to spend a few days with them near London. You will be very excited to go on this little adventure. But while you are there, you will start to notice your nan speaks to you differently than she does to your sister. You will have picked up on this before, but as you are now a little older, you will sense she has a favouritism towards her. It will feel cruel to you, and you will become very upset. By the end of the next day, you will feel isolated and run away.*

*You will learn as a child you are somehow unlovable and not worthy of your nan's love. You will come to realise you need to feel loved, especially by your family. Your pain as a child is no different to that of an adult with the same experience. You will carry the hurt, and it can break your heart, as mums and grandmas are supposed to love all with equal measure.*

*Jumping forward, those hurtful digs you will endure over the years will have you believe your nan didn't really love you. It will all be resolved though. When you are twenty-two, you will understand she didn't mean to hurt you. You will sit on her hospital bed and hold her hands in her final days. She will tell you how sorry she is for the way she treated you. You will both have tears, but your heart will brim with forgiveness.*

*You will learn to teach children that adults have their own problems and sometimes will put them on you. They don't mean to hurt you.*

*You will come to realise saying sorry takes courage and strength. Acknowledging your forgiveness is not only liberating; it also heals your heart.*

*At fifteen you will have to start wearing glasses and you will feel embarrassed. You will want to be more like your big sister. She will have lovely straight, blonde hair, a sort of 'Twiggy' look, whereas you will feel dowdy and unattractive. You will have beautiful, long curly hair, but will spend time trying to straighten it for you'll think this is how hair should be. One Sunday afternoon, a group of you will meet up and go to the bowling alley. There will be a boy there the same age as your sister and you will talk to him. He will make a flippant comment to you that your sister is prettier than you. Your self-esteem will drop again that day.*

*You will learn as a teenager your looks are what get you (boy) friends. You feel insecure about your looks.*

*You will come to realise what others think of you doesn't matter; it is how you feel about yourself that is important. Your real beauty is inside you.*

*Your first serious boyfriend will be from the local children's home. He will be the first to tell you how lovely you are. He will even give up his very pretty girlfriend for you. He will be good-looking and funny; you will feel for once that perhaps you are special and even attractive. You will have fun but come to realise he is a bit of a bad boy. He will take advantage of you on many occasions, but you will still get engaged at sixteen. Your parents will support your decision. You will soon work out for yourself when the time is right and come to know, deep in your heart, it could never work. You will tell yourself you are worth more. You will be nearly eighteen before you make the decision to end it, and it is going to be tough, but your family will support and protect you. They will love you no matter what. You will go on to make decisions and choices about what you really want.*

*You will learn boys do not always show respect; you must respect yourself first. You have an inner, intuitive voice, and you listened.*

*You will come to realise relationships are not always made in heaven. It is tough being a parent handling the challenges of teenager's ways. Despite what Mum and Dad felt about you choosing to get engaged, they loved and trusted you enough to let you work out what you wanted for yourself. They were always there to pick you up.*

*I want you to know, years later, you will meet him again, and he will apologise for the way he treated you. You will remain good friends.*

*At the age of nineteen you will get married. Your husband will be introduced to you soon after the break-up with your fiancé. You will enjoy a very different relationship. You will both work hard and buy your first home together.*

*You will have three beautiful children: Daniel, John and Julia. You will lose your first baby at 28 weeks; it will be a tough and painful time but one year on Daniel arrives. 21 months later,*

*John will be born prematurely. When he is only ten days old, the hospital will call to tell you to get there without delay, because he is deteriorating. But your faith will keep him alive, you have him baptised. He is going to pull through and you will be overwhelmed with gratitude for his precious life.*

*Despite a troublesome pregnancy, your daughter Julia, one of twins will survive. Your miracle daughter will be born prematurely in the back of a car. You will be brave and strong that night. At the hospital, you will be told she is cold and may not survive. You will believe if she has the strength to survive being born, she will have the strength to live, and she will.*

*You will be devoted to your children; your heart will burst with love for each of them. From the day they are born and throughout their lives, you will do anything for them. They will be your life and you will have reason to be proud of them all. They will gift you six beautiful grandchildren.*

*You will come to realise you are strong and can keep your faith in the face of adversity. You will know pain of loss, sadness, yet joy and happiness when it comes to having babies and raising your children. The love you have for your children is beyond measure.*

*You will learn to teach your children they are unique and special. That faith can move mountains. God has a plan for us all, and they must accept that whatever life brings, there is always a reason. They must endure their challenges, for they will make them stronger, but they will know you love them no matter what.*

*After just six years, your marriage will break up. You both realise the love is no longer there. As a Catholic, your parents will have real difficulty accepting your pending divorce. They will have their own battles about what people will think in the church community. You will feel a sense of shame that will leave you struggling. Going through the divorce will bring its challenges, and one night you will feel so low, you will not be thinking straight; you will just want to sleep and forget everything. Those whom you should have been able to talk to will either be disapproving or too young to understand. You will want the raw emotion, the pain and the hurt, to go away. It will be as if a lifetime of emotions are swirling in your head and nothing makes sense anymore. You will swallow pills to kill your pain. By some miracle, your new partner, Terry, will call you; he will sense something is wrong, for he will hear it in your sleepy voice. He will immediately respond and get the neighbours to break in; he will save your life. It will be a pivotal moment for you and your parents too.*

*You will come to realise, despite all the strength you had shown in the past by overcoming situations and supporting others with love and kindness, it seemed nobody was there for you. Your 'bucket was full', you could take no more. There is always a way, but taking pills is not the answer, for such actions have painful consequences for others. High emotions create impulsive behaviour. Life is precious, and there is no problem so big it cannot be overcome.*

*You will learn to teach your children: no matter how hard things get, you can get through. Mum and Dad love you no matter what. Be there for others and don't judge them by your own limitations.*

*You will discover the depth of true love with Terry, and you will remarry. It will be a joyous occasion. You will also remarry in the Catholic Church. The love you have for each other will encourage you to discover and become who you really are. Love will continue to be your driving force through the years, and you will go on to give so much of yourself to encourage and support family, friends or even strangers if they are vulnerable and needy. Some will take advantage of your generosity and kind heart. They will leave you feeling hurt, used, misunderstood, misjudged and put-upon. The trust you put in everyone will feel tested beyond measure. But do not despair, for you will have a special place in the hearts of so many more. You will be there for them with your loving kindness, words of support, encouragement, compassion, empathy or physical support at their times of need. You will support them as they turn their stress, trauma or overwhelming times around. You will grow older and wiser, tested by many life challenges, including financial hardship, grief, broken relationships, feeling overwhelmed, work pressure and much more. All these experiences will give you a unique strength, and you will become even more resilient, for you will learn much about life from your challenges, but you will promise yourself you will never again be broken.*

*You will learn to teach your children it is not the problems they will have to face in life, but how they deal with them, that is important. Stress is not meant to break you, but challenge you to find solutions, so you become stronger and can help others get through their challenges. People will love you for who you are, not for who they think you should be.*

*What you learn about yourself is that, although you hit rock-bottom, you turned yourself round and, from then on, stressful situations made you determined and stronger. The more diverse your life journey becomes, the more you learn about yourself, and stay strong to support others. You must look after yourself first. Love is so powerful.*

*You will enjoy many years with your husband and will always have his love and support so you can fulfil your dreams. You will be inspired and become inspiring, as you will discover your many skills, attributes and capabilities. You will have many successes, achievements and proud moments. You will study in your late thirties and, by the age of forty-two, you will achieve three degrees and take up teaching. You will work with young people for seventeen years and will come to discover how each child can be damaged by their 'history' and the limiting beliefs and indoctrination of others, including their family, friends and peers. While teaching, you will further study therapies including head massage and reflexology. As a yoga teacher too, you will become more and more interested in the well-being of others.*

*When you come out of teaching you continue to teach yoga which you love. You will come to a point in your life where all the wisdom, knowledge, skills and experiences you acquire are all part of God's plan for you. When you reach fifty-eight, you will choose not to retire, but instead to fulfil a dream and open a yoga centre for well-being. At this time, someone will share information that will lead you to South Africa and, there, you realise your life journey prepared you for something profound.*

*On return to the UK you will find yourself alone with no support. Your passion, however, will be strong enough to drive forward, despite the challenges you will face from others. Through your many experiences you discover the power of the human body and evolve the practice into something quite special. You will give hope to so many and empower them to transform their lives as they heal from their past and build resilience. You will be chosen to create a powerful message for the rest of the world. You will teach your message with a passion that never wanes, by freeing the body that holds physical, mental and emotional pain, the chains of the past can be broken. Everyone can set their children free, as you will your own.*

*You will learn to teach your children they must believe in themselves. They will do, and be, whatever their heart desires. That giving and receiving love is powerful; parents can inspire or destroy their own children.*

*What you learn about yourself is that, if you are passionate about something, no one can keep you down. You have achieved beyond your dreams and expectations. You will never stop learning. By breaking your chains with your practice, you set your children free. They learn something too; they can pass on to their children. You were chosen for something special; your diamond will shine.*

*Know that I love you Caroline for the special person you are to me. xx*

**What golden nuggets did you learn from your experience?**

I learnt my life, with all its twists and turns with each experience, was something I had to go through, for it was shaping me, and it all happened for a reason, forming my destiny.

Fallouts with others hurt, especially in families, and need to be healed soonest. Being there for each other, talking, trying to understand rather than walking away and allowing things to fester, is always the better option. But all involved have to want that too.

It took me a few years to accept myself for who I am. I was always thinking I was never good enough, attractive enough or clever enough. I eventually realised I am okay and I am worthy and clever enough, because the only one I have to step up for and be answerable to is me.

**What would you tell other women experiencing this?**

Whatever challenges you have been through, physically, mentally or emotionally, I want to reach out and say you are not alone in your suffering. No matter how dark life can become, or how low you feel, there is a purpose to your life. You are a unique and special person in this world, so keep going. Each experience is a learning experience, although you may not be aware of it, yet you will be strengthened by each one. You can heal from your past, have hope in your heart and you will become stronger and find your purpose. My amazing dad used to say, "You do not know what I feel unless you have walked a mile in my shoes." I have walked some miles, but maybe you have walked many more.

**What things would you have changed about your situation if you could?**

Knowing what I know now, I would have been stronger to deal with the behaviour of others projected on me, and not let myself get hurt. I would have been empowered to let go of the negative experiences and built my resilience from a young age. Knowing what I know now, I would have been able to support those people in my life who had suffered from life but took their problems out on me. Not just those with whom I shared my story, but others – family, friends, colleagues and acquaintances who challenged my love and trust. All were wounded by their own history, and in turn blamed or hurt me and, no doubt, others, as their way of coping.

My gratitude to them all for what they taught me about human nature; more than any textbook ever could.

**Any final words?**

We all have choices. Sometimes it is not the easy route that is the best choice, but trust that, whatever you face, you will come through stronger – if you want to! Everything will be fine in the end.

Love yourself, for you are special. Love will find a way to overcome everything. Love is free and we all have plenty to give, and everyone needs it. Trust your heart and trust your God.

You cannot take responsibility for others' behaviour. If adults cannot sort out their problems, sadly, it will be the children of the next generation who will be impacted the most. Listen to children, treat them with respect too, for they are our future.

Speak your truth.

**How can people get in touch with you and see the work you do?**

- Email: *caroline@treuk.com*
- Website: *www.treuk.com*
- LinkedIn: *https://www.linkedin.com/in/caroline-purvey-64235526/*
- Facebook: *www.facebook.com/treuk/*
- Twitter: *www.twitter.com/TREUK*

"I learnt that everything we go through is a gift. It might not feel like it at the time, but when you can reflect you can see, that these events and experiences are the things that make you who you are."

– Della Judd –

# It's All About Making Choices

### Della Judd

*Executive coach, writer, mentor and advocate for flexible working, positive leadership and team motivation in corporate settings*

What are you passionate about and how are you contributing to the world?

As a motivational, executive coach, leader and role model, I have been fortunate to have coached and mentored hundreds of people in the last twenty years in senior roles and am an advocate for flexible working and positive leadership.

I am passionate about influencing organisations to create a culture that enables people to work more flexibly, in a way that ultimately adds value to the business. It's great to see how people respond when they are trusted to work in a way that suits them, and to see the response from leaders who see that this can work.

My mission is to help create a corporate world where leaders treat people as human beings, as individuals, and where people at all levels can be trusted, respected and flourish at work.

**Describe a pivotal time in your life you wish to share.**

A big moment for me was when I was ten years old and my dad left home for the first time. I remember walking down my street after school and seeing my dad's car on the road, which was unusual because he would normally be at work. I sang *Daddy's Home* (the Cliff Richard song of the time!) to him as he opened the door, only to realise something was not right. Mum was crying and they told me that Dad was going to leave for a while and live in a flat for a bit. Mum was devastated, and my brother and I spent hours comforting her, sitting in the garden trying to stem her tears, helping her, not the other way around. During that time, she was often ill, and her dark moods increased. She'd been violent and created fear in our home for many years before this, but we simply flocked to her, to help her out.

Later, Dad returned to the family home, and I remember being so happy, that we'd be a normal family again, maybe Mum would be happier now?

After his return, we moved to a new house, to a new town. Everything 'appeared' to return to normal, but nothing really changed. I know that my dad found my mother's behaviour increasingly difficult, and the divorce happened later, when I was nineteen. By then, all of her behaviours were even more engrained, and my mum was more dependent on my dad and us children.

I experienced, first-hand, what happens when a woman is totally dependent on her husband – money, friends, social life. I think I decided then I didn't want that for myself. She simply collapsed when he left and had no self-worth or plans for herself. She tried to take her own life several times, and while this was a result of many issues, I saw a woman who had lived her whole life in someone else's shadow and so, when that person stepped away, she saw nothing left of herself. I saw, in those key moments, lessons that helped me realise I had choices in how I wanted to live my own life.

**Looking back, what made it such an important part of your life journey?**
I sometimes wonder what might have happened if my dad had actually left and my parents had got divorced when I was ten. Instead, he came back and we carried on 'as normal' for another nine years. This allowed my mother's behaviours to become even more embedded over those years, with her moods, violence, sulking and her standoffishness all increasing.

Looking back, I can see it made me self-dependent, determined and a little bit afraid to let people come too close. I bought my first house when I was just twenty-one – I had no family home to go to – and I knew I could do it and be my own person. This period made me realise families break up and, if you become too reliant on a person, you have nothing for yourself, and you can become nothing. This was really driven home during this period.

I have got a wonderful husband and family now, and I have let them in to my life, but it took me a while to realise I was quite different from my mum. I made deliberate choices to be different, to forge my own path, create my own self and value my own abilities. It was a lesson I learnt during those difficult years.

By learning I could make choices at this stage in my life, I jumped into my career with all my energy, with real determination I would not just roll over and let someone else control or define me. I grasped every opportunity I had and landed senior roles and managed large teams, all before I was thirty. I think this early part of my life meant I wanted to ensure I was 'good enough' on my own. I also learnt very clearly I wanted to treat people how I wanted to be treated. I knew from seeing mental illness, bullying and bad behaviour up close, how it felt. My intuitive and caring self was honed during this period, and I know this has helped me become a successful and inspiring leader.

**Based on the wealth of knowledge, wisdom and experience you have now, what would you like to say to yourself back then?**

*Dear Della,*

*You're so young to feel such fear; I know you are scared and terrified, let down horribly by the one person in your life you should trust the most. What I can tell you now, decades later, is that these events, these terrible fears, will be the making of you. You will be able to connect with people, understand people, and by using your intuition, understand and care for them.*

*Most of all, you will learn you can make choices and be able to inspire others, mentor others, show others they can make choices in their lives, whether at home or at work.*

*I'm sorry to tell you that, even before you are three years old, you will be subjected to your mother's anger. You are not going to* grow up to know the love you see in the films and read about in the storybooks.

As a toddler lying on the big bed with your knickers pulled down, being smacked and screamed at with your mother holding you down, you feel terror. Real fear, as the violence comes at you. I am with you, young Della. I can't protect you in that moment, but I am there, right by your side, whispering in your ear, telling you it will all be okay. This is your mother's terror, not yours to own.

Della, this violence will continue, and I am sorry to say, you will experience the fear of it and the actual violence itself for many years to come.

When you are about seven or eight, you will find yourself standing at the front door, dressed and ready to go to school. Your mother will look down at you and say, "You can't go to school like that." You have a black eye and she can't let you go out and be seen with the bruise on your face. She will let stay home and, on that day, you will be treated like a princess: jelly, cake and cuddles. This is a revelation. You will be rewarded for staying silent and hiding the truth.

This will make you feel special, but living with someone who is violent is like walking a tightrope – that you are learning to walk along at a very young age.

I want to tell you, so that you hear me, Della: you are not to blame, when she takes the bamboo cane and chases you round the house. You've not done anything wrong, you're just an everyday *kid, mucking about. You won't even remember what caused the violence, only the violence. That's because nothing you did was wrong, and nothing was worth the violent act. You didn't deserve it.*

*When you reach fifteen, like many girls of your age, you will play truant. It is your one and only bunk off school, spending the day with your two friends, sunbathing. In hindsight, not a sensible thing to do, getting sunburnt when you're supposed to be in school. Unfortunately for you, the school will be worried and call your parents, as it is so out of character for you to be off school. By the time you get home, your mum will already know. She will ask innocently, "How was your day?" and you will answer, "Fine."*

*You won't see the punch as it lands, but you will see the stars rise in front of your eyes as you fly across the kitchen floor. "Don't lie to me," she will scream. And you will know you were caught. She will draw out the punishment, so you will find yourself spending the next two weeks in your room, only allowed out for school or for meals. You'll get great at pop quizzes during those two weeks! Once again, you will be hidden from view with your shame.*

*Please know again, it's not your fault; most kids bunk off at school, and the punishment was unduly harsh.*

*As you get older, Della, you will learn more tactics to protect yourself. You will even take your friend home one time. Having mucked around, you get your school shoes and coat muddy, crossing the field that was out of bounds. You take your friend as protection. You fear your mother's reaction, so your friend provides humour and a comfort blanket.*

*You'll see a pattern as you grow up, of violence and of your mum cutting people out of her life. It will be a theme, her method of keeping boundaries, but also, for you, one of frustration. You are always held at a distance. No cuddles, kisses, hugs, no "I love you," no affection. It feels hard, you really want to care, and you do – you're a loving girl and you try to keep going back, apologising when you don't need to, caring for her when she is ill, when she sinks into depression. You will find yourself doing all the cooking, cleaning and washing. You do it all because you care and you're being a good, loving and kind daughter. You're there for her even after all the brutal events of the past.*

*I am so proud because, when you are eighteen, you will get a place at university. It is your dad that will take you to look around, and your dad who will drive you up on the first day. You will arrive with your bags and it will be your dad that gives you a hug goodbye. Your mum will just stand in the room, empty. She won't hug you or say she loves you. She will just leave, making you feel abandoned all over again.*

*But I want to tell you, it is here you find peace, new friends and create a new life, and where you will meet him, your rock, your best friend, your husband-to-be. This is where, aged eighteen and growing into your adult self, you start to realise you can make choices. You will start to see you can choose your friends, choose where to live, choose not to take on as many burdens from your family. It will take some time, Della; there are a few more lessons to learn yet.*

*When you reach nineteen, your dad will finally decide enough is enough and leave the marriage. Again, it will fall on you to comfort her and care for her. She will be devastated, as she knows no other life and hasn't planned for any other future. You will sit with her night after night talking, listening and consoling. When she breaks down, she will get depressed, unable to cope or comprehend what has happened.*

*And this is when she will try to take her life for the first time with alcohol and pills and, unfortunately Della, you will be the one to find her on the kitchen floor, the one to call the ambulance, that sees her taken to hospital. It will be awful, and you will be traumatised for a time afterwards, but you will get through it, coping with wisdom beyond your years.*

*Prepare yourself, Della, as she will try again and again, and you will find yourself slipping into a pattern of going back and trying to love her, because she is your mum. With each try, she will become more and more distant and withdrawn, and you will feel your own anger start to get mixed in with the hurt as you ask, "What about me?"*

*Yet, Della, although this is a trauma that will take you years to unravel, this experience will help you see people, truly see people, through their pain and their masks, and it will give you a greater understanding of mental health issues you will use in your career with great success. You know she is ill, and you now know about mental health, but it still hurts.*

*She will get better, little by little, after years of treatment and hospitalisation. But, I hate to tell you, she will remain distant, cold and uncaring. You will become frustrated each time she behaves this way, and will start to question how long you can keep going.*

*Violence appears again, Della, when, aged twenty, your boyfriend of eighteen months will punch you in the face, drunk, at a university ball, and this time you will choose you. It will take some time to make this decision; this man has been in your head for a long time. You get taken in by him, see his attention as love, like the behaviour of your mother. When he punches you, your friends surround you, telling you to call the police. You will say no, you don't want his life ruined by some drunken mistake. You will try to hide his behaviour, as you tried to hide your mother's. The next day when he comes grovelling on his knees, he will apologise. But you still won't feel strong enough to tell him no, not outright.*

*Eventually when term finishes, he will visit you on your home ground, and you will find the strength. You will remember a girl you worked with who turned up to work with a black eye, and that you said to others: "If someone did that to me, I'd be long gone." So, when he steps off the train to visit, you'll know this man is a bully. He doesn't love you. He was creating you in an image of what he wanted you to be. You'll tell him that night. It's over. And he'll leave the next day. Enough. You choose you.*

*When you return to university, you are free, happy; you will laugh and be yourself. And you'll fall in love, with a man who becomes your husband. You've known him for ages, loved him as a friend, a man who is kind and takes you out for drives and asks if he can kiss you. Say yes, Della, say yes. He is the one. He and his family will show you a new way. And, together, you will create your own family.*

*During the next few years, when you are getting ready to start your life with your husband-to-be, you will visit his parents and sister and you will see a new way to behave. You discover that other families show love, give out hugs and welcome you into their lives. You will find this a surprise, a revelation. All through this period, you will still be struggling to choose you, when faced with your mother's power over you. Despite the constant withdrawal and distant behaviour, you still want her love.*

*When you are twenty-six, you will be planning your wedding and during this period you will recognise you are loved by so many people. You have so many people who care. As Christmas approaches, you offer your mum yet another olive branch, a chance to show you care when you invite her for Christmas dinner, and she will reply with: "I don't want your fucking charity."*

*You will decide, in that moment, you have had enough. Enough of every single phone call ending in tears or fury or accusations. Enough of trawling through the past as she accuses your dad, and everyone else she claims is to blame. Enough of being rude to your partner and criticising your family. Enough of criticising your weight, telling you not to choose the purple dress because it will make you look fat. Enough anger.*

*You don't want to live in this state of anger and upset any more, so you choose. You choose love, your husband and family. You choose you, and I can't say it will be easy. Not many people say no to their mothers. But I want you to know it is a brave, brave decision. The right decision. And you will never regret it.*

*Ever.*

*You will feel sad, of course. Many moments will arise where you think that it would be nice to still be in touch. Choosing a wedding dress, for example. But let me tell you, Della, because of your brave choice, you let other people into your life. Your wonderful new stepmum, mother-in-law-to-be and bridesmaid go shopping with you, and you'll have a joyous day with these lovely ladies, a day of love, not criticism. Your wedding day will be full of happiness and love surrounded by everyone who loves you. With the birth of your two wonderful children, you realise at their birth and naming ceremonies how many people in your life care for and love you. You choose that for yourself. You are brave.*

*It will be a theme that I see throughout your life as you make decisions, and they will serve you well. You will choose a new job to be nearer your children after your son becomes ill, choose your family after a restructure at work, you choose you time and time again. You choose your life balance and your family.*

*But I will warn you that when your health ails you time and time again, Della, you will ignore it for a while. I urge you to take more notice. Migraines are a blight and, while you will seek lots of treatments and people over the years, the main thing you need to look at is balance and reducing your stress. Keep an eye on it.*

*Although suffering with your health will give you great empathy with others and allow you to champion health, balance and flexibility in the workplace, you will also spend a lot of days in darkened rooms and miss out on too many social occasions. So, I'd advise you to take care, ease up. Choose you as much as you choose your family, your friends and your work. When you choose you, you become a better wife, mother and friend.*

*As I look back at you, as that frightened girl and traumatised young woman, I know all those experiences shaped you and made you who you are today. I want to remind you that you are successful, funny, empowering and inspirational, with great ideas. You are all those things because of all the choices you made. You're amazing.*

*Yes, you were neglected, abused, asked to parent your own parent, but you made the choice to step away from that toxicity and not subject yourself to it any more. What you learnt is to have instinct, intuition, compassion and love. These are the gifts you gained from these experiences and let me tell you – you will use those skills every day, in every interaction in your work.*

*You will be angry too, Della. Later, when you've made your choice to follow your own life, you will be angry at her behaviour. You'll be angry she was not a loving mother. You'll be angry she let you down, and the hangover of her treatment comes back time and time again, playing tricks on your mind as it tries to protect you later in life.*

*I know what I am about to say won't help you or ease your pain but, looking back at this point, I can tell you she wasn't a happy person. Rumours came later she'd had a troubled past herself. Not an excuse but, maybe, a glimmer of understanding as to why she never mentioned her past.*

*You were expecting and craving the love every child should expect from a parent. You were abandoned and spent years building a wall around yourself, showing people you are okay, not hurt. You won't let people be close to you easily. I understand that, Della; it helps for a while.*

*Don't let the anger eat you up. Seek the help you need from others to let you talk about it, release it, reframe it and help you focus on the future of your own life.*

*Break down that wall, don't build it up as high, don't hide behind it for too long, because you have a message, you can help others, and you need to allow the wall to come down. Allow people in and your light to shine out.*

*You'll need to pack up the past, taking only the learnings and gifts you took from the experiences with you.*

*You've got important work to do; it needs no baggage. Leave that unnecessary stuff behind. Share your gift of understanding people, your intuition, empathy, kindness, your intelligence and wisdom with others. Share it as a wife and mother, as a leader, businesswoman and influencer, storyteller, mentor and writer. Take these gifts and look forward.*

**What golden nuggets did you learn from your experience?**

I learnt that everything we go through is a gift. It might not feel like it at the time, but when you can reflect you can see these events and experiences are the things that make you who you are.

**What would you tell other women who might be experiencing this?**

You have choices. It might not be obvious right now, but someone out there can help you. You can walk away from people, even your own mother. You don't need to put up with bullying, violence or criticism; you can create your own new life. You find other people who will love you for who you are. People say that 'blood is thicker than water' and I would disagree – many people I consider my real family are not blood-related. Find your own tribe of people who love you.

**What are some of the things you would have changed about your situation if you could?**

I experienced a lot of ill-health, and I would have taken notice much earlier. My migraines were symptoms of lots of stress held in my body, a reflection of the stress in my life. They basically had to keep on knocking me over until they were so bad I had to take notice. I'd listen earlier and take more action to look after myself.

**Any final words?**

I feel this experience of sharing my story has been life-changing. I know some of my closest friends will not know some of the things I have shared here, because I have been so determined to keep everything inside and to show I am okay. But this process has shown me you have to let it out; don't hold on to the past. These experiences have shaped me, and I am proud to be who I am and know everything I learnt is what makes me the woman I am today.

**How can people get in touch with you and see the work you do?**

- Website: *www.dellajudd.co.uk*
- LinkedIn: *www.linkedin.com/in/della-judd-50256942/*

"Never take your life for granted. Life is an experience and whether you believe that you only have one life or come back again and again, you need to cherish each moment that you have."

– Leanne Pogson –

# When the World Stood Still

### Leanne Pogson

*Survivor through her own resilience, international author, speaker and founder of the award-winning Leap, helping others grow their businesses with the support of their people*

What are you passionate about and how are you contributing to the world?

Every year I see thousands of businesses losing time, money and good people simply because they didn't include a HR specialist at the beginning when creating their business growth strategy. Massive financial losses to any business has a negative impact on customer service, unnecessary stress for the business owner and, ultimately, irreparable damage to their reputation that often leads to closure. One in five businesses close every week, and I believe it really doesn't have to be this way. People are an integral part of any business; whether they work for you or buy from you, people are the key. It's not rocket science that if you treat people the right way, there will be mutual respect and professionalism.

I want to change the way the world thinks and reacts to HR; the letters themselves and the mindset. Proactive not reactive, supportive not obstructive, develop and grow, not hire and fire. The journey doesn't start and end on day one, it lasts forever ...

**Describe a pivotal moment in your life you would like to share.**
The world stopped and in one moment, my life changed forever. It was the first time I felt completely lost, broken and out of control. I've had moments before where things have happened, but never properly listened to the message the universe was delivering. This time, though, I had to listen as I was slapped really, really hard.

You may not believe in the power of the universe, you may think it's all about your life, your choices, your responsibilities; but just sometimes there are situations where these are taken away from you, where you cannot control or influence what happens. They don't happen often, but when they do, the world and your life changes forever, and you have to decide how you cope, manage, live with it ... or perhaps not. And we are back to your choice, the never-ending circle of life and action that goes round and round.

This is what happened to me. I was in an accident. I was driving and someone died. I didn't choose to kill someone, to rip apart a family, to feel the guilt, the pain that followed. But it happened. And I have to live with it for the rest of my life.

I passed my driving test when I was seventeen and drove pretty much every day. I had jobs where I would spend days in my car, driving up and down the roads of the UK; I even drove in Europe and America. I was comfortable behind the wheel of a car and really hated being a passenger. I liked the control and I was a good driver.

A couple of rear-end shunts in the past (obviously not my fault), but this was something else.

There are things that you expect to see on a main road at night, and as an experienced driver, I was aware of most things. But this night I was not expecting a mobility scooter travelling on the road, unlit, no reflective clothing, completely unseen until the split second before I actually hit him. I later found out his vehicle was set to 8.6 mph, the maximum his vehicle could do. I was doing 50 mph when I hit him. It doesn't take a genius to work out what happens at the point of impact.

He died, I survived.

It wasn't just that night that changed my life path, but the events that followed, the slowness of a process, the lack of support.

I was interviewed briefly at the scene, tested for drugs and alcohol; I was then told I could go and to wait for a call. I have a practical head. As a career I help people; I understood the need for a procedure.

When I had a phone call from the police several days after the accident, asking if I wanted a second post-mortem done, I mean, what do you say? I was told to get a solicitor. I had contacted my insurance company about the accident and, after this call, phoned them again. Like many of you, I am sure you pay for legal protection on your insurance. Guess what? It doesn't cover a solicitor in these circumstances, so I had to literally beg for help, to be eventually told they would need to ask a senior manager. I felt so small and defenceless.

Eventually, twenty-five hours later, I was told the "great news" they could appoint me a solicitor until the police interview. The solicitor was nice enough, but it wasn't about me, the person; I was just a case. He told me not to speak to the police at all without his agreement; I mean, they are the police, there to help you, aren't they?

I was interviewed by the insurance company; that's a different department from the actual accident one. And over five months later, I was interviewed by the police formally. I was told the delay was because they wanted to do a reconstruction of the accident and interview any potential witnesses.

Of course, I understand the need to check, but it was a very, very long time of heartache, misery and soul-searching. In that time, I had surrounded myself with close family, good friends and business colleagues, visited the doctor's to seek help. Simply put, though, there is a lack of help out there. Mental health waiting lists are lengthy, months long; doctors give you pills. Pills to help you sleep, to help you cope, to stop your brain ... pills, pills and more pills!

Someone said to me that such a delay was sloppy policing, but I don't blame the police; there simply are not enough of them to deal with such a crisis. Their role is to support the family of the victim, not the person who could be the cause of the accident. I mean, I can speak for myself, but the other side is gone; he has no voice, so support goes to the silent party. It's not right, I am a victim too, but today, that's the way it is. And there we are, back to your choice. Accept the status quo, or do something about it.

And here I am, taking control back and doing something about it!

**Looking back, what made it such an important part of your life journey?**
There is no coming back from such an experience. I cannot make him live again, take his place or turn the clock back. But I can share what happened and how I coped.

It doesn't need to be an accident in the same vein as mine; but there needs to support for those involved in accidents from all sides. When I went to the inquest, the family had a police officer with them, someone from family liaison. Nothing like that is provided to the driver of a vehicle.

Yes, I understand in some cases, fault can be attributed to one party or another, however most cases are not as clear-cut. Support needs to be fair, consistent and available to everyone involved.

This whole experience shook me to the core, made me stop and think about my whole life and the path I am on. I still want to help people, but actually to truly share how to manage when you experience such a massive experience is where I am now. I have sought out my own help, learnt new skills to help me cope and now I am fully able to share what I do, my story, and to guide people through their experiences.

Based on the wealth of knowledge, wisdom and experience you have now, what would you like to say to yourself back then?

*My dearest Leanne,*

*Here I am writing back to you at the tender age of forty-eight. It seems strange to write to you from only a year away, but there is good reason. You will be involved in a car accident that will not only be traumatic and scary, but will ultimately change your life.*

*Everyone who knows you knows how much you like to be in control; and while you will skirt along the edges of the rules, you seldom if ever cross that red line into morally or legitimately wrong. Rarely do you give control to someone else.*

*As I write to you, I need to tell you there will be a moment when you won't be in control; shit will really happen and, above all, there will be nothing you can do. The universe decided that, on that night, your path will be changed forever.*

*Leanne, as you read on, please do not be afraid, and know that I tell you the truth; everything will be okay. What will happen is your destiny and, as distressing as it was, there was some inevitability about it, as the universe placed you on this path for a reason.*

*Do not be afraid of the challenges you will face as you come to terms with what has happened. But you are a brave, brave woman who, like a phoenix from the ashes, will rise stronger, a warrior* who will survive an ultimate test of faith, determination and bloody-mindedness.

On that fateful night you were your normal, practical self. The pragmatic rule-follower, always taking breaks on long journeys and, on this day, you stopped to have something to eat.

You are buoyant; the GB Davis Cup team had won the tie and you sing along to the radio as you get nearer home. You are almost home, your hubby, Chris, driving in the car behind you. You know he is okay, too.

It's 8.30 p.m., you are travelling along the main road. The speed limit is 50; it's dark and overcast. There is an occasional glisten on the damp road from the lights of other cars, and you dim your lights so they are not blinded. Passing through a village, most of the houses are unlit or away from the main road. There is no street lighting. You travel past hedgerows, trees, and notice a pub to the right of you, set back, dimly lit from external lighting.

Then it happens.

Just after the pub, you will be in an accident. A split second before the almighty bang, you caught a brief glimpse of something, you just won't know what at that time.

Everything moves in slow motion. At the glimpse of whatever it was, you instinctively slam on the brakes. A huge bang reverberates *as the car hits this object in the road. Apart from the sound of the radio, there is no other noise, the air palpable, and all at once you realise you have hit something.*

*Then you scream, "FUCK!" as a figure flies through the air in front of you, away from the car, the shape of a person glowing in a white hue as they glide horizontally through the air, landing on the ground in front of you.*

*Struggling to get out of the car, realisation smacks you; you have hit someone.*

*You have killed someone. A human being. You did not see him. You jump out of your car, almost being run over, wanting it to be you, screaming to your hubby, anyone, to call an ambulance.*

*Your world will stop, Leanne. You won't want to step forward to see what has happened; you will want the ground to open up and swallow you whole. Your head almost exploding at the thoughts you have.*

*But you will not comprehend at that time ...*

*Seconds later, still trying to call an ambulance, you're fumbling, trying to unlock your mobile, desperately shouting into your phone, "Ambulance, I need an ambulance. I didn't see him. Please, I need an ambulance." Somehow you are sat on the grass, its cool wetness beneath you, your phone still not connecting. When it finally does, the voice is telling, no, demanding, you go to the body in the road.*

*Someone goes running past you. A man kneels in the road by the person on the ground. Pieces of plastic are scattered around you, a flip-flop, a battery ... and all at once you know this person was in a vehicle, a mobility scooter.*

*The phone voice insists you go over to the body. The Good Samaritan is talking to him, telling him to hang on, starting CPR. In tears, crying into the phone, "I don't want to, someone else is there, why do I need to?" Consciously, you know his soul has left his body, that he is gone. You see the cut on his leg, just split open, no bleeding, and a bare foot, but you do not see his face.*

*Leanne, please don't go over; you do not need to see his face, to have that imprinted on your memory. Later, you will know who he is and what he looks like when he comes to you as a vision when you are in a deep meditative state. You won't recognise him then, but he will tell you how much he forgives you, and in your heart, you will know this.*

*You take a step forward, toward the figure on the ground, still crying and challenging the voice. The Good Samaritan takes your phone, places it on the ground in front of him and, placing it on speaker, he starts counting loudly as he does compressions.*

*You stand sobbing, hysterical, directionless, noticing your husband has started directing traffic. From behind, someone takes your shoulders, saying she is a nurse. She gently hands you to a man who holds you in his arms. He is telling Chris to take you to his house. You don't want to go, but he gently manoeuvres you down the path to his kitchen, onto a stool, asking if you want a drink. You know he means alcohol, but don't take it. Leanne, you know it isn't right, and you don't want it anyway. Chris appears by your side and holds you. The man makes you both a hot drink instead.*

*You won't remember how long you sat in an embrace, but you start to feel a pain in your side. Outside, the sirens of emergency vehicles will be heard, the reflections of their blue lights around you. You will sob again; not knowing what to do or say. There are dogs in the house, two Labradors who will sniff you and lick your fingers. Instinctively, you will stroke them.*

*You mention the pain, and a paramedic appears by your side. You say to her you deserve the pain. But, Leanne, you do not deserve to be in pain. Instinctively, you will feel you need to be punished, but you don't. The paramedic goes away, saying to call her back in if the pain gets worse.*

*You mutter to Chris how sorry you are, that you didn't see him, over and over again. He hugs you and tells you not to worry, it was an accident.*

*A lady appears and opens her fridge, pulling out a bottle of what looks like whisky. She offers it to you, you decline. The pain is back, harsher than before, and the lady, seeing the pain in your face, will try to move you to a more comfortable chair. You ask to use their toilet and, in this hiding space, you sit, sobbing, seeing yourself in the mirror, reliving, second-guessing what, how, why did it happen?*

*Over and over again you do that, convinced you are a murderer, that it's your fault. You eventually throw water over your face and return to the lounge. More talking; the road is dark, treacherous and accidents are frequent, but nothing will take the guilt from you.*

*More paramedics come in; one asks how you are feeling and about the pain in your side. Connecting you to a blood pressure monitor, you will be asked about your medical history, medication you take. There are four paramedics near you; one is talking, telling you your blood pressure is extremely high; she smiles at you and explains she isn't surprised, asking you to try to relax.*

*Leanne, I know it will be hard to do, but try to take a deep breath. As you speak, she will write. You realise then, not all the paramedics are for you; gazing around, you listen. They are exchanging car keys, talking about driving different vehicles.*

*You hear mumbling behind you, briefly aware Chris is talking to the couple who took you in. You notice the looks between the people there and feel like you are wasting everyone's time; you have no cuts, no broken bones, you are bruised but still you feel the pain is justified. Why the furtive looks between the people there? Your senses are heightened and you wonder, "has he died?"*

*After many hours, a policeman comes in. He says he may be a while yet and asks the homeowners if they know where the victim lives. They explain he lives in a shared house behind theirs; they say they see him most days going to and from the pub.*

*It feels like forever before he returns. He cautions you, explaining why. "Of course," you say, knowing there has to be a procedure. Taking out his notepad, he starts: "Can I have your full name and address?"*

*He tells you that you can leave if you want, you are not under arrest, but you don't want to, you say, "I just want to help." You notice how quiet the room is, the paramedics gone. The couple creep into another room and silently close the door. Just you, the policeman, and Chris. You still see the blue lights dancing around the room, silently reminding you of what happened.*

*He is gentle with you, explaining you have to be breath and drug-tested. You agree. A breathalyser is proffered to you; you breathe into the tube until he says stop. Silently, he put the test on the table. He asks you to open your mouth and takes a swab from your cheek. Again, he says nothing as he places that test on the table.*

*He sits down.*

*Asking you what happened, he prompts you in some areas for more information. "Where have you come from?" "How long have you been driving?" "What speed were you going?" "Did you see him?"*

*Answering each question, you feel like this is a dream, like watching a movie from a distance. Sobbing softly, you are all too aware the kindly policeman is just trying to find out what happened. There is* a split second of relief when he tells you your tests are clear, but you knew they would be. He takes your mobile, explaining it needs to be checked you were not using it at the time of the accident, but not to worry, it will be back with you in a couple of weeks.

You hear his radio; muttered comments being sent to him. He ignores it for a while but eventually he responds "All received, understood." Desperation will creep into your stomach; lurching, you start to feel sick. You will know what it is.

He then asks Chris similar questions. "How far behind were you?" "What did you see?" Chris explains he saw a piece of plastic coming under the car and thought it was part of a golf trolley.

And then he puts his pen down. He looks at you and says, "There is no easy way to say this but ..." You finish his sentence, "He's dead, isn't he?" He replies "yes."

Sobbing again. "I've killed someone, I'm a murderer." Chris tries to calm you down, the policeman says it just seems to be an unfortunate accident. He explains to you the scene has to be checked before you can leave. It makes no difference; trapped, you have nowhere to go. You feel like your life is over.

The policeman talks to the couple then leaves. The couple try to make small talk, telling you about other fatal accidents there; you appreciate them, they are lovely people, trying to make you feel better, but you won't feel comforted – you don't want to be *another statistic. They tell you he seemed to be a very sad man; that is no help. Later you think it doesn't matter what type of man he was, he's dead.*

*You feel cocooned, watching the blue lights reflecting on the walls around you. Chris disappears outside and returns, saying: "As we walk out, don't look left." You know your car is there. You hug and thank the couple as you leave the safety of their house.*

*You step out into the cold dark air, a sob escaping as you see your car. Chris gently guides you to his car and you notice the police looking, then turning away. You feel that it is because they blame you. Chris's car is facing the opposite way you had travelled. He tells you the roads are closed, and you have to go a different way home. At each junction, there is a police car, blue lights flashing. You feel you have caused so much trouble. Repetitively, you say: "I'm so sorry."*

*Chris is told not to leave you. In the early hours when you get home, you will not sleep. "I've murdered someone, I am a killer," on replay, looping over and over in your head. In your pyjamas, you lie on your bed, but you can't sleep. The dark is scaring you; unwilling to shut your eyes, you watch episodes of a 1970s sitcom. Chris is asleep; you get up and go downstairs. It's 3 a.m., the telly is on, its drone comforting; you sit and stare into space.*

*You are in shock. In your head, you don't know what has happened, what to do, where to start? "Everyone will hate me, I'm a killer. I killed a human being. I will be judged for what I did, I will go* to prison. I can't see anyone." You want to vanish. The thoughts rattle around in your head.

My darling, it's okay to feel like this. The trauma you have gone through is colossal; don't try and fill in the blanks. Your memory is a wonderful thing and will protect you. There is no need to go in to the minutiae of what happened. This will be uncomfortable; you are someone who likes the detail, but it's okay, you are safe.

Chris gets up at 5 a.m. He tells you the police are going to come that day and he will stay at home with you. Tea is made and left untouched; you hug a glass of water instead. Willing you to eat something, Chris makes some toast. It sits for hours until you finally decide to eat some.

You were told you would have your mobile back in a couple of weeks. That is not to be, Leanne; your phone would not be returned for six months, so you will need to be patient.

There was no call that day. The police didn't arrive, so Chris called and left a message. An hour passed and finally the phone rang. No one was coming. They were very busy. There were just not enough police, you understood, but deep down you were screaming as you wanted it to be over.

For the first few days after the accident, please know, Leanne, it is natural to go through a lot of emotions. There will be an end, even if it doesn't feel like it, but trust in yourself and the universe will support you.

*You will learn patience, Leanne; you will understand and you will learn to carry the anguish. You are a victim too! But know this: you are a survivor, a warrior, your journey on this new path just beginning ...*

*Love and hugs always.*

*Your older you,*

*Leanne*

**What golden nuggets did you gain from this experience?**

Never take your life for granted. Life is an experience and, whether you believe you only have one life or come back again and again, you need to cherish each moment you have.

It goes without saying when you experience trauma, you learn who will stick by you, no matter what. But it dawned on me that, since I started my own business, I have never been so supported, so loved than I am now. When I was employed, I am sure there would have been support, but in all likelihood, this would have come with conditions. There would have been a timescale, there would still have been expectations to deliver on time, to achieve goals. But now I know that truly the people who are in my life – my family, my friends and business networks – were there as one, not just with me, but for me as well.

If there is anything to share, it is that you don't need to bear any tragedy alone. People in your network may not be able to take the pain away, but they have experience that will help you manage, teach you techniques that can help you relax, use the pain to grow.

**What would you tell other women who might be experiencing this?**
Never be afraid to say how you are feeling. Remember those loved ones around you.

And others will help. I will help. You just need to ask.

**What are some of the things you would have changed about that situation if you could?**
They say that hindsight is a wonderful thing, and it goes without saying I wish it never happened. But in this case, I am not sure it would have helped anyway.

Looking back, I could have chosen not to drive that evening, stayed in Scotland for an extra night. Chris was in the car behind; if he was in front, it could have been him. It could have been someone else who had the accident. And actually, I know it could have been. A near miss the night before reported to the police with the same mobility scooter at the same location in the dark could have spared me this heartache.

But in reality, it was me. My path wouldn't have changed if it hadn't been. The experience, not great, but my life is more blessed and rich because of it.

I now know the procedure used and I now know this procedure is not right. I know changes need to be made and I know I will be there leading that charge.

**Any final words?**

I am a survivor. Life's agonies can make you stronger. You have a choice; follow my lead, be a survivor too!

**I'd love to connect with you. Here's how to find me:**
- Website: *www.leaphr.co.uk*
- Email: *info@leaphr.co.uk*
- LinkedIn: *https://www.linkedin.com/in/leaphrltd*
- Facebook: *https://www.facebook.com/leaphr.co.uk/*
- Twitter: *https://twitter.com/LeapHR1*

"Surrender and let go. When people and things are removed from your life there is always a reason and a bigger picture we can't always see. Practice gratitude for the positive elements that remain. This is a world of balance- for every bit of pain, pleasure can be found."

– Lilli Badcock –

# Finding Freedom in Faith

## Lilli Badcock

*Transformational confidence coach*

W hat are you passionate about and how are you contributing to the world?

I am passionate about reminding others how powerful, magical and needed they are! I use the power of music and specifically singing to rebuild lost confidence and realign people with their purpose and joy. I also work intuitively with those souls who have been called to create epic change in the world. I help them to find clarity in their mission and to step forward boldly and shine their light for all to see!

**Describe a pivotal time in your life you wish to share.**

One of my most pivotal moments came when I lost my voice. As a professional singer and vocal coach, this was far from ideal. I had no idea at the time how the events leading up to that moment had affected me. I also had no idea what doors would open as a result!

I know now the physical loss of my voice was a representation of the way in which I'd been hiding from my own power. I had allowed the projections and opinions of others to dictate who I was and how I showed up in the world.

**Looking back, what made it such an important part of your life journey?**

If I hadn't lost my voice when I did, it would be easy to believe I may never have started to explore this spiritual path I now find myself on, the path that has now led me to help others as they navigate their own awakening. Of course, I now know and believe this was always my destiny. But the voice loss jolted me into action for sure! Had I not experienced all I did, I would never have been able to meet my soul-aligned clients where they are at – knowing they have something powerful to offer the world but riddled with anxiety and frustration and unable to gain the clarity they need.

As clichéd as it sounds, I really do believe it was necessary for me to experience the path I did to truly understand the magnitude of the work we are all here to do.

**Based on the wealth of knowledge, wisdom, and experience you have now, what would you like to say to yourself back then?**

Quite simply, I would have reminded myself that I am always okay. I am infinitely loved and supported at all times.

Faith in this truth is all I ever needed.

*Dear Elizabeth,*

*I am writing this note to you right now as a forty-one-year-old version of us.*

*It really has been quite the ride! You are right to feel as excited about life as you do.*

*You are a pure and beautiful soul capable of astonishing things, and you have been blessed with a family of warriors who will lift you, love you and inspire you every step of the way. This is rare, Elizabeth, and don't ever take it for granted. When your dad tells you you are amazing, clever and talented ... BELIEVE him! Oh, and watch your mum. She is a lioness whose fierce loyalty and capacity for love will be one of your greatest lessons, and the thing you treasure the most. This will serve you well in the years that follow.*

*Your story is one of FAITH. It is a full circle you are destined to complete. At the time of reading this, you are still safely encased in your bubble of love and security. You have only ever known the miracles life is capable of bestowing and your heart is full. At this point, you don't even realise there IS a bubble!*

*To you, this is life, and it's wonderful!*

*But bubbles are fragile. When they burst it can be a hard fall. What I'm here to share with you is the journey you are heading for, into a world beyond that safe and secure environment you call life. There are shadows that lurk right next to the light you are so familiar with and, for a while, you will feel afraid and lost.*

*But you are never lost. This is, perhaps, your greatest lesson of all.*

*As a schoolgirl, you endured years of bullying, and countless times you would feel like you had no voice. You would let those people walk all over you, but you would stay silent, always craving the quiet life, never wanting to rock the boat. Come to think of it, you never really felt like you fitted in. You always felt ... different.*

*You would be twenty-eight before you stuck up for yourself for the first time, and the shit really hit the fan! As a result of this, and what you THINK you learnt at the time, you feel that when you put yourself first, bad things happen. You were hurt and confused by those who couldn't see your light and tried to bring you down. You didn't understand what you'd done wrong and, in the process, you learnt to modify who you were to keep others happy.*

*But the true lesson was far more powerful, and what you ACTUALLY learnt is that it doesn't matter who you are or what you do. There will always be those who don't get it, and that's absolutely okay!*

*But let's talk some more about that pivotal moment, shall we?*

*You were nineteen years old and already, for years, singing had been your passion and salvation. Many happy hours were spent locked in your room, singing at the top of your lungs to Mariah*

*Carey, Whitney Houston, Mary J Blige and Aretha Franklin, among so many others.*

*It is at this age you first met Gabriel. He really gave you the gift of confidence and strength when it came to your voice. He had your back and believed in you even when you didn't believe in yourself. Over the years that followed, he became a solid mentor in your life and someone you trusted implicitly. You have so much to thank this man for, even now. So much of what you treasure and hold dear in your life is thanks to him and what he guided you to.*

*Shortly after starting your singing lessons, you were invited to join the choir Gabriel ran. Little did you know when you first walked through those doors, what lay ahead were some of the best years of your life! You made life-long soul connections, you found your own voice and made the transition from part-time karaoke singer to full-time professional singer and, later, vocal coach! The choir family became the first group you ever truly felt part of. Those people became the MOST important people in your life.*

*When your marriage broke down, it was your choir family that pulled you through with no judgement. They rallied around you and formed the support network and stability you had always craved in what was otherwise a very confronting time. When the opportunity arose with an associate of Gabriel's to open your own studio and take over the running of the choir you'd grown to love, you grabbed it with both hands. You packed up your entire life, including your cat, and made the move to Salisbury to make your dreams happen. With nowhere to live initially, you put your cat into care and lived out of your car for seventy-four days. You had all your clothes in cases and your shoes were in the boot. Your parents definitely thought you'd lost the plot, but you didn't care! You were doing what you loved, and you were surrounded by the unshakeable love and support of the friends you'd made. You were back in a bubble where you felt so safe and so supported that nothing could shake you. You were completely unstoppable!*

*But challenge and conflict were lurking around the corner. You see, in your excitement and glee at being asked to open your own studio, you signed a contract in absolute faith without properly reading it. You agreed to terms that were not sustainable and, very quickly, you began to struggle. You weren't working with as many clients as you needed to keep your head above water, and you were paying most of what you earned back out in royalties and other business expenses you hadn't taken into consideration.*

*The truth is, you weren't ready to run a business. You had no knowledge of what you were doing or how to make it work and, while you loved working with your clients, the rest of the business was failing. This was the first time you truly began to struggle with money. That was something that would stay with you for years to come and almost completely bring you to your knees.*

*You knew you couldn't continue in this way, but you were so afraid to speak up and say so. You so appreciated the opportunity you'd been given and you still loved and adored Gabriel and didn't want to let him down. You also felt like it had all been fate and it was your destiny to do this work, so you couldn't understand why it wasn't working.*

*But it wasn't working, and you were paying the price for ignoring your intuition.*

*It got to the point where you had no choice. You couldn't continue in that way. You knew what you had to do. After an initial meeting with Gabriel's associate, where you'd voiced your concerns and been told there was nothing you could do, you called another meeting and told him to his face you could not and would not continue with the agreement. You sought the advice of a professional with regards to the contract and learnt it wasn't a legally binding document and not worth the paper it was written on. The meeting concluded swiftly, with little drama, and the associate left.*

*At this point, you felt shaky, but certain you'd done the right thing. After all, if it wasn't working for you, it couldn't have been working for him either, right? And besides, it wasn't all lost. You still had your friends, your support network and everything you'd built over the years. You would continue to teach for them, but just not run your own branch of the studio. It was all going to be okay, right?*

*Wrong.*

*The phone rang. It was Gabriel. He was LIVID! What followed was one of the most upsetting and traumatic conversations of your entire life. Yes, even to this day. You were told what you'd done was unethical, that you had no conscience and that, because of you, an elderly man (his associate) was physically ill with no financial support (you were told multiple times you were, essentially, his pension.). When you asked if you could work from their other studio, you were told it wasn't possible and, at that moment, the bonds were severed.*

*In the moments that followed, you cried so hard your housemate, who was upstairs, thought you were laughing. When you called your mum, you couldn't make a sound to speak and she thought someone had died. You felt completely alone, and didn't want to be here any more. It was one of the only times in your life when you've truly felt like that.*

*Sadly, it would get worse before it got better. In the fallout of the situation, the band you had helped set up ceased to exist because one of the members was related to Gabriel and his associate. You lost so many of the people you thought were your friends, and you realised the truth, that most of what you had considered to be real had in fact been superficial. The bubble had well and truly burst.*

*In the years that followed, you struggled. You didn't know it at the time, but you carried the guilt of what happened and the belief you were a terrible person, and certainly not someone who would ever be worthy of real happiness and freedom. You believed the life you created out of the remnants of your bigger dreams were all you were worth.*

*You became trapped in a cruel contradiction. You were living the dialled-down version of the life you'd always wanted – so near, yet so far. You grew to believe others could win, but not you, and that you should be grateful for what you did have and not ask for more.*

*You became so small, so apologetic, so silent, and you almost completely disappeared!*

*It's no surprise really that you crashed and burned the way you did.*

*In fact, the signs had been there for a while but, typically, you had brushed them aside and carried on regardless. It was going to take something SERIOUS to slow you down!*

*When you first lost your voice, you didn't panic. Losing your voice had become a regular occurrence. You believed it was because of the regularity and force with which you were using your voice. After all, you were teaching so many hours every day and then performing on weekends, with never any opportunity to rest. But the days rolled by and one week turned into two, then three and at that point you started to believe you would never sing again. You also convinced yourself singing was not for you, and that you shouldn't be teaching it either. After all, you'd wrecked your own voice; why would anyone pay you to wreck theirs too?*

*And there it was. Your very own miracle! Because, for the first time in your life, you experienced what it truly was to lose all confidence. You experienced anxiety so severe that, some days, you could barely leave the house. Of course, at the time it felt like a complete breakdown. But I'm here to tell you that, my love, it was your ultimate breakthrough! It was the catalyst for everything you would become and everything you were always meant to be! Shedding the skin of who you thought you were was always going to be messy. But you made it through!*

*You always knew you would. Deep down, you always knew you would.*

*Losing those people in your life felt painful for a long time. The memories and fear of that experience have come back time and time again, and it's taken a long time for you to come through to the other side. But I can tell you that you get to experience what true soul-alignment feels like. You get to meet people who expand you in every sense of the word, as you do for them. These are your people. All those times when you felt like you didn't fit in, you just didn't know where you 'belonged' was never in just one group or in one place.*

*You see, what I've learnt at this point is that we are tethered at the soul to those people we are here to impact and change. It was never about changing the world single-handedly. It was never necessary to be liked by everyone. This mission we are all on is a group effort. All you ever had to do was be yourself because, when you do that, your soul shines like a beacon to every person you came to help.*

*The hours and hours of time spent ignoring your own intuition and desires were only ever going to bring you the chaos that followed. Please understand, this was just your higher self, getting your own attention!*

*What I'll say next feels almost pointless, because I won't be telling you anything you don't already know. But you really ARE magic!*

*The power you have felt since as far back as you can remember is absolutely real.*

*At this point, it truly feels like you went on a journey, because you started to believe it was necessary before you would be worthy or deserving of the prize, whatever that looks like for you. But you were already worthy! You were already deserving! You were BORN this way! The heartache, pain, struggle, hustle, the campaign, crusade, was only one route in. The easier path was always available to you.*

*So, above all, I want you to know you're right and you can TRUST yourself. I also want you to know you are stronger than you know. You will hear a saying later on, which states that God never gives you anything you can't handle. This is absolutely right. But there's more to this. You can handle it all because you are NEVER alone. That calming presence you can feel all around you right now will never leave you, although at times you'll think it has.*

*I'm writing to you from the other side of that episode, and I can tell you the whole experience was STRENGTHENING your faith. It enabled you to refine what you knew in your heart to be true. It was all conspiring perfectly, so that when you entered your forties, your beliefs would be rooted in KNOWING. Isn't it funny you always looked forward to being forty? Well, now you know why! While it is almost impossible to prepare you for what lies ahead, I want you to remember to keep the faith. The path is not always clearly set out in front of us, and we don't always know how a situation will resolve. But resolve it does. Never forget you are infinitely loved, and are being guided every step of the way.*

*Over the years that follow, you will meet people from all over the world who have lived truly remarkable and, in some cases, heartbreaking lives. You will be a tower of strength for these people, and your capacity to love and understand will be shown to all. You will become known as someone with the power to heal through your essence and energy. For that reason, you will have a large circle of friends and acquaintances, and doors will open for you left and right. This will be a far cry from the loneliness you felt aged six, when you didn't seem to fit in. You will realise fitting in was never the aim but, rather, standing out! You will never be short of opportunities, and you will come to see you were never alone.*

*However, as you meet more and more people, you will start to feel guilty your own life was so blessed. You will feel as though you need to hide, and you will even start to wonder whether you endured pain so terrible you'd blocked it from your mind. But this isn't the case. Your life HAS been blessed, but with very good reason. How do you think you will hold the space for everyone who needs you without that solid grounding to begin with? This idea that before you break through you must break down is not absolute truth. It is just the common path for so many humans and, now most people believe this is the way, it must be.*

*You are different. You always were. Never lose sight of this!*

*Finally, there is one more thing you have to know. It's true you are a soul on a divine mission and are living a remarkable life with the purpose of helping countless others to do the same, and wake up to their true purpose. And to support you in your human form, you were given a gift: your voice. Your voice has the power to heal, the power to move; it is the calling beacon to every soul on earth who needs what you have.*

*Your love of music and singing is something that will stand the test of time. And, eventually, it will be how you bring people together. You will be a walking, talking example of what is possible when one allows themselves to be soul-led.*

*You have the tendency to overthink situations, and you are unbelievably hard on yourself, – something that will get worse before it gets better. But, Elizabeth, please never ever forget who you are and why you're here. Trust your heart. Be led in faith and don't ever be afraid of that power you feel inside you.*

*After all, this is what you signed up for! Let your light shine and be the example to the rest of the world, for this is truly how positive change will come.*

**What golden nuggets did you learn from this experience?**
It's not possible to fail, and growth is always available.

Intuition is a thing, and mine can always be trusted.

**What would you tell other women who might be experiencing this?**
Surrender and let go. When people and things are removed from your life, there is always a reason, and a bigger picture we can't always see.

Allow your emotions to be felt. Don't be afraid of them. There is healing to be found in the darkest of times.

Practise gratitude for the positive elements that remain. This is a world of balance – for every bit of pain, pleasure can be found. Seek the light in every dark corner, but don't be afraid of the dark.

Question what you believe to be true. There is always another perspective.

Trust your biggest dreams. They are meant for you!

**What are some of the things you would have changed in this situation if you could?**
At the time, I may have changed my choices, with the ultimate goal of changing the outcome. Of course, now I can see exactly why things had to play out the way they did and so, in that respect, I wouldn't change a thing.

I guess, if I were going back today, I would ensure I had the strength and knowledge of faith I have today. I would want to know it was okay not to be okay and that I was never alone.

**Any final words?**

Remember who you are. Seek those moments of peace in the chaos to sit with your greatest dreams and remind yourself every day you were born worthy of all you desire! Love yourself HARD! Bear witness to every imperfection and every 'wrong' turn and know that you are always okay.

Surround yourself with those people who see your light and allow you to shine bright, so you can live the life you came here to live. Do this for others and allow it for yourself, for this is truly how we will change the world.

**How can people get in touch with you and see the work you do?**

- Instagram: *https://www.instagram.com/lillibadcock*
- Facebook: *https://www.facebook.com/lillibadcockconfidencecoach/*
- Website: *https://www.thelilliclub.com*

"Believe in yourself and never let anyone put you down. You will grow stronger and learn the true value of your worth. Never compromise on loving who you are and honour yourself. Forgive others and you will find the release in your heart you have been holding for so long."

– Tracey Harrowven –

# Shining Bright at the End of the Tunnel

### Tracey Harrowven

*Member of the YES Group Leadership team. Passionate creator of inspiring poems, quotes and handmade arts and crafts, empowering people to let go of overwhelm and enjoy the present by embracing their creativity.*

**W**hat are you passionate about and how are you contributing to the world?

For many years I did not believe in myself, and found I had lost hope but, through the help of others, I realised I have so much to live for. Turning my life around, I changed the way I see and think, which has made a positive impact on my life and those around me. Through my writing of inspirational, empowering and heartfelt poetry, I help others to see their true selves and that life can be truly amazing. My mission now is to help touch the lives of as many people as possible, and restore love, happiness and self-belief back into their lives.

**Describe a pivotal moment in your life you wish to share.**

For me to tell you my story, I need to share several pivotal moments in my life that are interconnected.

My first moment happened at a very early age when I was bullied and teased by my younger sister and others. I needed to have an eyepatch, and then glasses, to correct my eyes. The bullying and teasing was focused around how I looked and, being so young, I didn't have the courage to fight back. I never realised how much this would impact on my life, but it continued to rear its head time and time again, a pattern of not being good enough, rejected for who I was.

Then came my school years. I was bullied, abused and targeted for the way I looked. It's surprising how lonely you can feel, even with people all around you. The pattern of bullying continued throughout my school years and into adulthood. I soon realised I didn't feel safe anywhere. Even home, which should have been a safe haven, was a place of wondering what I would be blamed for next. The thing that kept me strong was knowing I was a good person.

Getting married and having children was my dream, but this also ended with emotional heartache and rejection. Meeting my present husband gave me the respect, love and attention I knew I deserved, allowing me to live my life in an abundance of happiness and love. Sharing my journey with him by my side has given me so much to live for.

I realised life is about choice and, as you get older, family are the friends you choose for yourself. This discovery has been very important in my life, which has given me the strength and self-belief to overcome everything I have been through to become the person I am today.

**Looking back what made it such a pivotal part of your journey?**
Each pivotal moment came with its own challenges. Being bullied, abused and rejected by others made me stronger. It helped me to forgive those who hurt me. It made me realise that, although you are born into a family, you don't necessarily have to get on. You will all follow your own paths in life. Letting go of the pain and hurt I had carried for so long allowed me to learn how to put myself first and love the true me.

**Based on your wealth of knowledge, wisdom and experience you have now, what would you have liked to say to yourself back then?**

*To my dearest Tracey,*

*I am writing to you at the grand old age of fifty-five. I know this must seem very ancient to you but, believe me, it's a great age to be.*

*I want to tell you, how proud I am of the lovely, beautiful little girl you are who has a heart of gold. You will need that wonderfully big heart and the strength and wonderful qualities that come with it, to overcome many challenges and rejections in your life. But, like everything you do, you will do it with no complaints and take it in your stride.*

*Although you have loving parents and siblings, things will not be easy for you in the family home. In life you will experience bullying, abuse and rejection, not only from your family, but others too. But you will overcome all of this, as you are a strong little girl who knows what's right and wrong, and this will inspire you to help others.*

*You will have to start wearing an eyepatch as your eyes cross over, and you can't see clearly. Don't worry: even though it will feel strange at first, you have to wear it, and you will still be as gorgeous as ever. This will get your eyesight back on track, and when your new glasses arrive, you will put them on and the world will now seem so much brighter and clearer, apart from that little black cloud that is your sister. The bullying from her will start now, first with teasing about your glasses but, pretty soon, it won't matter what you do, because you will always be her target.*

*Your sister will see you as an easy target, as you never fight back. You are not the sort of person who likes fighting and confrontations, instead happy in your own company, amusing yourself by drawing, reading, writing and making crafts. Tracey, you're very good at them, and I'm so proud of everything you make.*

*As you get older, the bullying from your sister will increase; always up to mischief, trying to put the blame on you and your siblings for anything she does. Your parents won't always see what is going on but, deep down, you know they know who is to blame. They won't like punishing you all, but will think that this is the right thing to do. They won't realise how much this will affect you, but they never meant to hurt you.*

*I know you feel let down by your parents a lot, even though you understand the reasons behind their actions. Being the good girl, you will always go along with it to keep the peace, in the hope one day your sister will curb her selfish ways and behave. But you will have no idea how devious and hurtful she can be, so please watch out.*

*I know you feel left out and deprived of attention and love from your parents, and this will follow throughout your life, as your sister monopolises the attention. You will find sanctuary in the fact you know you are very good girl who is polite and enjoys helping others, especially your mum.*

*There will be times when your sisters are fighting over the top of you, and you just carry on drawing, minding your own business. It will make you chuckle inside; if only they could see how silly they are. You know in your heart your mum would have loved them to have been just like you, an easy-going child, but that is not always a good thing.*

*When you start school, you are so excited but, being easy-going and little for your age, you will again become an easy target, for your sister and other children too. They will be so mean and bully you. I know as you go through the day trying to be brave, even though you're hurting and upset inside, you will try your best not to show it. You are so resilient and will learn quickly how to rise above it all, even at this early age.*

*I want to tell you, sweet and loving Tracey, as you go into your teenage years, your body will change, and your dad will jump in on the act, calling you thunder thighs, inch-high (as you remain very petite throughout your life) and other names. Tracey, he doesn't mean them nastily, but I know it will hurt you deep inside. You must remember that going into puberty is a big step towards adulthood, and you are neither fat nor short; your body is just developing into that a beautiful young lady (and remember, all good things come in little parcels!).*

*Throughout your school years, the bullying will continue. They will send you to Coventry (meaning they won't speak to you or let you join in any of their conversations). Over time you will turn this to your advantage, becoming stronger and enjoying the peace and quiet this brings. You will decide not to tell you parents what's happening at school, as you don't want them to be disappointed with you. (I believe they probably know, but thought it best not to say anything. I'm sure they were looking out for you, even if you didn't realise it).*

*You won't find schoolwork easy, but will always do your best. Your sister will call you stupid when you ask for her help. So, you will shut yourself off from her and, with determination, you will do everything yourself without any help. But I want you to hear me when I say this Tracey; it is okay to ask for help, it is okay to not do it all alone. Because, when you try to do it all alone as you grow older, it will tire you out and make you physically and mentally exhausted. There will be wonderful people out there that want to help, so know you are not alone.*

*You will move out of the family home at the age of nineteen, and your younger sister and brother will be spoilt rotten by your parents. They will do and experience things you would never have been allowed to do when you lived at home. It might feel like you* are not part of the same family. It's okay for your paths to go in different ways and, I can tell you, your path will be awesome.

By the time you turn twenty-two, Tracey, you will have two children. I know how much having children will mean to you as they will be your world. They will be so beautiful and fill your heart with so much love and joy beyond your wildest dreams. You will be such a wonderful mother and it will come so naturally to you. Your love for your children is endless, with pure devotion to them. You will get so many compliments on how well-behaved and polite they are.

Alas, the future you planned will not be so. You will find yourself raising your children alone after your husband walks out. I know being on your own with two small children was not part of your life plan, but you will tackle this problem head-on in the quiet and self-controlled manner you always have. You will be so courageous. Your mum and dad won't come around much and will always have things to do if you ask them to babysit, which is hard, as you never ask them for help unless you really need it. However, where your parents lack, you will have friends who are always there to help without judging you.

This time will make you feel even more shut out by your family, but know this: you are a tower of strength, an excellent provider for your children and a fantastic mother and friend. Tracey, although these times will be hard, within three years you will meet your new husband and he will sweep you off your feet and fill your home with so much love and affection. He will be a breath of fresh air. Your children will love him too. Tracey, you deserve this happiness and, for the first time, you will have someone in your *life who's there for you. You are a wonderful lady. Your children will flourish having both of you in their lives.*

*When your son is thirteen, he will decide he wants to go live with his dad. This will break your heart, but you know you have to let him go. At thirteen he thinks the grass is greener on the other side. How wrong he will be. Tracey, I want you to know it will not be your fault when he goes completely off the rails. It will also not be your job to save him, but instead you will learn just to be there for him, no matter what he does, loving him unconditionally.*

*When your daughter is sixteen, she too will move in with her dad. Yet again it will break your heart to see her go, but you can't stop her. In your house you have rules and, in her dad's, there are none, and at sixteen she just wants to go to the nightclubs with her friends. Tracey, I want you to know, you did nothing wrong; children grow up quickly and believe they know best. I know you will feel abandoned by her as she doesn't come around unless she wants something, and hardly ever calls. You are a great mum and can try your best to support her even though your relationship is distant.*

*Over the coming years, your children will disown you. Although this hurts, know that you had no control over what they did, from the day they moved in with their dad. You did your best, Tracey; loving, nurturing and helping them as best you could and always being there for them.*

*I want you to know that, no matter what you will go through in your life, people often won't see your beauty, worth or greatness.*

*Those that bullied you will take away your belief, for a while, as they try to strip you of your greatness and you will feel rejected by those people who should have been there for you. But Tracey, life is what you make it, and in 2015 you will meet a true friend. She will be like a sister to you, what you always imagined a sister to be. You will even look alike.*

*Meeting her will change everything. You will feel accepted, and her husband and children will treat you as if you are part of their real family. You will have so much fun together and it will make you realise that, although blood is thicker than water, family are those people we choose for ourselves. You will start to remember who you truly are, as these friends show you unconditional love. They love everything about you, as you do them. Through their eyes you start to see the wonderful person you are. Your heart starts to fill again with love, and you feel so empowered, that you can achieve anything you put your mind to. You will start creating again, like you used to all those years ago when 'sent to Coventry' or trying to hide away from the battleground of your siblings. You will write poems around the things that happen in people's lives, to show them there is always light at the end of the tunnel and they can have a better life.*

*Tracey, I want you to know, you can't change your past; it is what it is, but life is for living now. My hope for you is that it is full of love and happiness with people you love and who truly love you for who you are.*

*I love you so much, my beautiful girl. xxxx*

**What golden nuggets did you learn from your experience?**

I learnt that from a very young age I should have put myself first and loved myself for who I was. Although I was bullied, abused and rejected by family and others, I have learnt to forgive and have grown so much stronger having had these experiences. I never underestimated the person I had been for fifty-five years, but now I have the strength, empowerment and inspiration to live my life to the fullest, ensuring I love myself, filling my heart with happiness and joy and surrounding myself with people of my choosing, who love me as much as I do them and appreciate me for who I am.

**What would you tell other women experiencing this?**

Believe in yourself and never let anyone put you down. You will grow stronger and learn the true value of your worth. Never compromise on loving who you are and honour yourself. Forgive others and you will find the release in your heart you have been holding for so long. Now is your time to shine.

**What are some of the things you would have changed about your situation if you could?**

The only thing I would change would be having had the courage to stand up to the bullies and ask for help. Other than that, I feel I have gained so much knowledge, strength and empowerment throughout my life to be able to achieve whatever I set my mind to. It also allowed me to choose the people I want around me, to bring love and happiness into my life as much as I do in theirs.

**Any final words?**

Let your heart shine out and believe in yourself. You have so much to offer others who will always be there for you. Follow your dreams and make your life a true reflection of your heart.

**How can people get in touch with you and see the work you do?**

• Facebook: *https://www.facebook.com/tracey.harrowven*

"The best life lesson I have learned so far is that we always have a choice even when it looks like there are no good choices to choose from. The hardest choice doesn't mean it is the worst. The fact that you are consciously making a choice already gives you freedom."

– Olga Brooks –

# I Chose Me

## Olga Brooks

*Founder of The Return, Inspiring Guide and a leader to the restoration of femininity, wisdom and power within. An immigrant, a mother of two boys, energy healer, teacher on spirituality and femininity.*

**What are you passionate about and how are you contributing to the world?**

I am on a mission to heal the feminine. Having gone through divorce with two children, I realised how vulnerable women can be, not only during the period of divorce itself, but after too. And this is where my purpose, admiration and inspiration comes from.

My true passion is the feminine essence; that inner beauty inside every woman, that gets forgotten and, in many cases, disrespected while going through life's storms. I help women to rise up in their inner power and beauty, by combining spirituality and knowledge of the deep feminine essence, bringing them to a place of understanding and discovery of who they are. I went through healing myself and know how important it is to become whole again to begin a new chapter in life and share a heart with the world around.

My vision is to provide women with essential information of what feminine energy is and how it transforms lives and the world. I guide women to heal that part of femininity and return them to a place of wholeness and love.

**Describe a pivotal moment in your life you wish to share.**
There are times in my life, and everyone else's, when we know looking back that if the experience had not happened, we would be somewhere else, and our lives would not be the same. But these moments shape and change our lives, and here are mine.

The last one happened only two years ago. I was looking at my psychologist's pointed fingers as she said: "You have two choices. First, the problems you have now, or the problems you will have after the divorce. You pick." Nora is a wonderful therapist from my church; she is sunny like California itself. Being with her in a room for forty-five minutes gives you joy and relief all on its own. But before I go into what I am planning to tell you, let me tell you the story of how this forty-one-year-old woman from Russia ended up at the psychologist's office in the United States, looking at the fingers of no good choices, and no possibilities but to live a life in stress, fear and poverty.

I left school at fifteen years of age, because that was the norm in Russia, and moved to another town to study to become an accountant, like my mom. I was a good student, able to turn my hand to everything and anything: Sport, acting, singing, playing a musical instrument, sewing and performing. However, schooling had its down side: bullies, rapists, looking over my shoulder wondering who was around the next corner. At the age of eighteen I graduated with a degree in economics and accounting and secured a well-paying job at the nuclear power plant.

In the nineties, massive changes happened in Russia, bringing many uncertainties and chaos at some point. Money in the government disappeared and people were left, often working for months without a paycheck. Many families lived on the produce from their gardens, eating mainly potatoes, cabbage, apples, pears, berries, herbs, cucumbers, onions and tomatoes. But I lived slightly differently; having bought my own apartment at age nineteen, I was independent and considered well off.

So, when my old schoolteacher asked if I would be interested in marrying an American man, I said no, although the thought of exploring the world and having a life outside Russia sounded appealing. At the age of twenty-two, I realised I couldn't live the way I wanted to in Russia; my brother had been killed, beaten to death by teenagers while he was walking home at night. I knew for sure Russia was not a safe place to live and definitely not a good place to raise children. So, I decided to go for a safer life, a life I knew nothing about, I couldn't even speak the language, but was determined and ready to widen the horizons of my existence. That marriage lasted less than a year.

When I met my second husband, I felt at peace as he respected me. He knew why I had come to the States without asking confusing questions since he had lived and worked in Russia for some time and knew the situation there. Having spent four years together, he proposed, and I said yes. However, in the car going to the church in my beautiful, self-designed blue wedding dress, with calla lilies in my hand, I heard a voice in my head saying it wasn't meant to be. I pushed the voice quickly away and focused on the life I was building. Sadly, fourteen years later, I found myself in front of a judge asking for a divorce. I had been tired for many years, nurturing and taking care of the children and, as often happens, our marriage got lost along the way. I also got lost; I didn't know who I was anymore or my purpose. At forty-one, I found myself alone and scared more than ever before. I feared the unknown.

**Looking back, what made it such a pivotal part of your journey?**
As I walked through life, it felt like a stranger to me. I felt like a stranger in a new land, a stranger to my husband, a stranger to myself. I realised eventually it was a gift I had been given, an opportunity to really get to know myself on a deeper level.

The choices I made brought me to the place of understanding about others and their struggles and pains. Through being small and powerless, I learnt that making empowering choices would give me absolute power, so I made the choice to be whole again. And through the healing I went through, I found my passion.

What made me utterly unhappy created a total flip in my life, becoming my friend and a lesson filled with knowledge and practical steps for the life of love and personal growth to share as a gift with others. It allows me to teach my children that tough choices are not always bad, but sometimes necessary to encourage and build us up.

**Based on the wealth of knowledge, wisdom and experience you have now, what would you like to say to yourself back then?**

*My dear wonderful girl,*

*Yes, you were dear and wonderful since the moment you were born. Your name is Olga, Olya, Olechka. You were born into a middle-class family, like most of Russia in that generation. Your parents work hard at the nuclear power plant and have done since it was built. Your town is very small and most people that come move from the villages to build a new future. Communism called for that. Yes, I hate to break it to you, but you live in a communist country.*

*The generation you will grow up in will work hard, pitching in together for our country's greatness, and most children growing up during this time are unsupervised, with the Communist Party teaching them far more than their own parents did. As you grow up, you will encounter many situations in which you can't do much as a child, and you will feel guilty for wanting to raise your voice to say "NO". From the age of five, you will sense the danger all around you, even when it is invisible to the naked eye.*

*You will believe from a young age that there will be a special man for you. A man who would protect you, so you would no longer be afraid of the dangers around every corner, of rape or abuse. You believe in your heart this man will offer you a deeper connection and support, only to discover that this man, your man, will not be found in Russia.*

*What you will experience instead is the danger that lives within masculine power. Where you expect to find love and protection, you will find fear and evidence of your own physical weakness. Your father, who loves you very much, will try to remind you how strong you are. He will want you to learn martial arts, to be strong physically, able to protect yourself, as he knows exactly what you need protecting from. You will feel sad you weren't able to do it at that time. But let me tell you, you will be wearing a black belt in karate with your two sons someday. And you will do it not from the place of fear, but from a place of strength instead. Oh, yes, you will have two beautiful baby boys. This is your wish, and it will come true.*

*But before we get into the joys of motherhood, let me walk you through some of the parts of your life, and get you ready for some challenges you will encounter.*

*You are an independent girl and will practice that skill from a very young age; always seeking freedom for yourself and others, able to handle many things. Leaving your parental home early, you will be exposed to life's lesson of protecting yourself and your close friend from the cultural immorality of the male generation in the town where you will spend three years studying.*

*You will often be scared for your body and your dignity while listening to the 'colorful' wording of the young men who want to break you mentally and to rape your feminine soul. But you won't show your fear, in fact you won't even blink; how are you so strong at only sixteen?*

*You will, however, become aware of everything: Who is around you, which way they are going, where you should turn. You are going to do so well. However, be careful of the shining knight when walking home in the pouring rain; a man will offer you a lift home. You have seen him many times before and, as you sit with him in the car, he will try to talk you into getting a visa to explore the world and visit Turkey. You've never travelled out of the country at this point, and this will sound exciting to your young soul seeking freedom. But you will listen to that inner voice that says "No". Years later, you will learn he was shot for selling pretty girls as sex slaves into Turkey.*

*You will be committed to your work, even though you won't really care about the numbers. You will show the older women you work with that life can be lived differently. Most of them are overweight, suffering from back pain from sitting all day for years crunching numbers. Your presence will be like a breath of fresh air. They will love your jokes, spirit and attitude. They will be truly scared and happy at the same time when you announce you are leaving Russia to live in America.*

*Yes, you will follow the recommendation from one of your teachers, going to Moscow to meet potential husbands, and in that moment everything will change. In a beautiful peach dress that your friend made for the occasion, you will walk into a hall full of beautiful women. Hundreds of them, of different ages, sizes, colors and shapes, all looking for a way out of Russia.*

*But you are different than most of them. Life is good, you don't need to run away, but instead are choosing a safer world. As you watch the situation unfold, you hear that little voice in your head say, "This is your chance and you should take it," as you are presented with three interested suitors. Everything will work out as it was meant to and, six months later, you will be land on American soil.*

*It won't be easy though, Olga. You will still be grieving for your brother, beaten to death on a walk home one night; your premonition of danger around every corner coming true. Even after you learn conversational English, you will find yourself lonely and trapped because there is no connection between you and your new husband. He will fear you and believe you to be unpredictable. So, he will decide to get rid of you through the law system in America and get you deported. But have faith, little Olga; the highest justice will think otherwise. You will find out very early it is wonderful to have a law system that works, but it might not always be on your side. You will discover the communist and the democratic system have their own scary similarities and pressures.*

*During this period, you will learn so fast; how to drive a car, which way to go when all the roads look the same. In nine months, you* will already have a job at the mall; not bad for a young girl who spoke no English when she arrived.

Eleven months later, you will be signing papers to be separated from the man who brought you to America. He knew what he was doing, serving you those papers, but unfortunately you will have no idea and, briefly, will become an illegal alien in your new country. It will be very scary. You will feel like you are alone in the whole universe. You will be presented with two choices: Stay illegal or go back home.

You fully understand you must protect yourself from the system to stay in the country. You will hope the Russian lawyers will understand what you are going through and use their knowledge of the law to help you stay in this country. But these are the same guys from the town you had escaped from. They promise help but instead abuse their power, to take what they want. You will feel unsafe again. You will be aware you could say yes to the millionaire who wants a pretty housewife, that would help you, and you would have the safety you seek in him. But you will know this is not what life is all about.

You long for a real relationship, where you have a deep connection to grow together, a meaningful life you can teach to your children. This is your dream. You will realise this is the only dream you have had throughout your life. Or maybe it was just the dream that was available to dream, considering where you came from? However, you will believe it is possible. And you will meet the person who *will offer you another chance at love. This time, you will take the time to see what you are getting yourself into; a man with a loving family. With his parents' help you will find a great lawyer, who's more like a fairy godfather, and in one immigration court sitting you will become legal again.*

*For many years you will feel that life is so good. All things are possible. Your creativity will bloom. You will work as a nursery teacher. It will be fun to learn proper English and see the culture of America through the eyes of the young. This will help you so much in bringing up your own kids. You will take art, dancing and acting classes, rediscovering your talents.*

*But I want to tell you, you will be side-swiped and derailed for about two years when, at the age of twenty-seven, you will have a stroke. You will be a survivor. You will listen to that inner voice yet again and know everything will be okay. You will have to go through this to experience the supernatural and learn about the human brain, the body and spirit.*

*I am not going to lie and say this will be a breeze; it will be a terrifying time for you. You will be alone in a hospital, confused, in pain and uncertain. Here you will meet your guardian angel and experience a supernatural phenomenon. Your dad will tell you over the phone you are strong, and you will believe him, even though you are unable to get out of bed on your own. You will recover and feel grateful for the support during your continuous recovery, for the man who stuck by your side. A year after the stroke, he will propose. You will have a beautiful, intimate wedding* with your mom by your side. But, many years later, it will be like a flashback in your memory. While being driven to the church as a princess bride, you will hear that inner voice again saying, "This isn't meant to be," but you will just answer: "Too late. I am on my way and everyone is waiting." And off you will go.

You will become a proud citizen of the United States of America while carrying your first child. The cracks are beginning to show during your first pregnancy. But you will think for the next thirteen years things can be worked on, until you hear yourself saying to your husband, "I want a divorce". The words of your mother-in-law will keep booming in your brain: "Co-exist for the sake of the kids." An awakened voice will cry: "I can't. I can't live my life like I don't exist. I can't teach my boys that there is no life in my life. I can't be stuck. Life is so much bigger than my pain and my struggles. I won't. I can't." This won't be an impulsive decision to leave your husband, but a decision that will be right for all.

For many years you will live in pain, believing you have no other way. Even though you will have these beautiful kids, after putting them to sleep, you will feel utterly alone. Although all of your material needs will be catered for, your heart will be in pain and your soul will be empty. And that is where you will meet yourself once again

Through this kind of disconnect in your relationship, you will find the way to return to your authenticity. You will realise it is not your husband's fault. You will take responsibility for yourself and stop blaming your husband. From feeling nothing, you will come back, so powerfully, to love life. Yes, you will spend some time in the darkness questioning who you are and what the meaning of life is. This pain will be enormous. You will stop going to church and to your therapist. You will understand you need to figure it all out on your own.

But there you will meet God, the creator, who hasn't been far away or deaf or blind. He was right there in you and you will find him inseparable from you. And you will realise you were never alone, that the creator of this universe was a part of you from the moment you were born. Everything you go through will not break you; it will point you right back to your wonderful self. And that is where all the magic will begin.

"What is it you want?" You will ask yourself this over and over, and your answer will be big, as big as your life. "I want connection. Deep and meaningful. That will make this world a better place."

And you will finally feel at ease for not being judged for your thoughts, words, emotions, desires, requests and feelings. You will be in love with the freedom of being you. You will remember all those internal talks you should have listened to, respected and followed.

The future is scary, but you will listen to your inner guidance and, through that, you will know life is so much bigger than the illusion of fear. And you are so much bigger than being a housewife.

*I know the responsibilities of creating a beautiful life for your children after the horror of a broken home will be enormous. You will admit that is the scariest time in your life. You will be afraid of the system, but you will do an outstanding job of protecting yourself and your children. Because of that, your passion to protect, teach and share wisdom with other women will be born.*

*You will leave the house you nursed your children in and create a beautiful new home for them. It will take some time for your kids to adjust. You and their father will make sure to minimise the damage. You will take them through some tough lessons so they start respecting you, your house rules and respecting themselves, but it will be worth it.*

*You will show the boys how much you love them by showing them life is not about pretense or misuse of power. Life is about love and about you. The true you. You will promise to teach them things that will propel their lives to greatness. Because of your choice to climb out of that dark hole and work on opening your heart, your boys will receive a blessing for many years to come. They will be loved and nurtured so they become great men. Men who know how to love, how to be strong and vulnerable, how to love and respect their wives. You know it is your job to teach them that, and you will do it diligently.*

*Going through such difficult times, you will learn amazing things. When you feel all alone in the big, wide world, you will learn that all emotions are observed by your higher self, by that part of God within you. You will feel her presence in you and remember you were never alone and the light of the brilliance inside was never dimmed; you just couldn't see it for a while.*

*You will believe it is important for others to see your light, and it will hurt you to the core of your being when you learn many can't. But even if they can't see, it doesn't mean it isn't there.*

*Remember, for some people, it will be too much, and it will feel like a threat to them and they will reject you. This will be painful to you, but you are a crystal-clear, refreshing brook of water to those who need a smile, understanding and a second look at life. You will meet those who see your light, accept and treasure it. You will learn along the way everyone has a choice, and how to respect people's choices, as you will make your own. It's only in those moments of struggle and pain you will start to see the true value of who you are and build a deep, real relationship with yourself, the one you had forgotten, almost destroyed, but the one you ultimately found your way to return to.*

## What golden nuggets did you learn from your experience?

The best life lesson I have learnt so far is that we always have a choice, even when it looks like there are no good choices. The hardest choice doesn't mean it is the worst. The fact you are consciously making a choice already gives you freedom. The hardest choices I have made have stretched and strengthened me. Inactivity to not make a choice breaks and weakens you. So listen to that voice inside you, as it is your true guide that I have learnt to listen to and trust.

**What would you tell other women who might be experiencing this?**
At times when you feel utterly lonely, please remember you are never alone. That voice inside you is the one which knows everything, and it will guide you to the depth of your soul. It will show you the way you should take. But you are the one to make that choice. Learn to listen to that voice.

**What are some of the things you would have changed about your situation if you could?**
If I could go back in time, I would love my children so much more. I would give them my attention and many smiles, which I haven't given them due to my inner sadness. I would not change anything about having my children, which means I would go through this again to give them life.

**Any final words?**
Life is so beautiful and has great meaning when you live every day with an open heart full of love to give, and the space to receive the same back. And that means living as your true self and being authentic. My hope for you is that you make the choice to live an authentic life by being a true you.

**How can people get in touch with you and see the work you do?**
- Email: *info@thereturn.live*
- Facebook: *https://www.facebook.com/pg/ thereturntomyfeminineself/about/*
- Instagram: *@thereturnllc*

"This whole experience was a healing process. Although it still feels like it was the darkest moment of my life, without it I wouldn't have found my identity, I wouldn't have discovered who I really am. I would have still been hiding behind my fears and limitations, imposed or self-imposed, denying my soul's purpose: to be happy and at peace with myself."

– Adina Oltean –

# The Slaying of the Beast

## Adina Oltean

*A blessed Romanian single mum of an amazing teenager,
founder of the Consciousness and Guidance Centre and
The Legacy Creation Series global movement, Therapeutic
Counsellor, Reiki Master, life student and passionate advocate
for enabling people to become the best version of themselves.*

**W**hat are you passionate about and how are you contributing to the world?
Over the last decade, I have coached hundreds of individuals to increase their confidence, self-esteem and self-worth to create profitable coaching programmes and sustainable online businesses.

It's a phenomenal experience and life gift to be part of the impact. It's being created all over the world and I have learnt that the more people I help, the more people are being helped in so many deeper ways.

My vision is to see millions of people inspire and support each other to live an enriched life, and for the way they live it to be a legacy in itself.

**Describe a pivotal time in your life you wish to share.**

Even though my story is about an event in 2014, it started ten years earlier, in 2004. At the end of February 2004, I gave birth to my beautiful baby boy. I was so excited to be a mum. It was one of my dreams to be a young mum, as I had always felt I had suffered from the age gap that existed between me and my father, who had me when he was forty-four.

My happiness was short-lived for two reasons. Firstly, my son was born small and sick. Secondly, my father died a week later.

My family chose not to tell me about my father immediately after giving birth, instead believing it was better to wait until I felt stronger. However, work colleagues called me to express their condolences and, in that moment, I discovered my father had died. This plunged me into emotional shock I didn't manage to heal, and was compounded the following year when I found myself fighting for my son's life when he developed a throat tumour which required two surgeries in two months. Then, three years later, I divorced his father and we both moved to the UK.

The event I am sharing with you is the healing period of my ten-year, undiscovered post-natal depression.

**Looking back, what made it such an important part of your life journey?**

I was born in the early eighties in Romania, which is a small country in eastern Europe. I grew up in a magnificent town called Sebes, located in Transylvania. I love my town and consider it the most beautiful town on earth because of the Red Ravine, which is unique in Europe. It's like a small version of the Grand Canyon, a place where, legend says, thieves hid their stolen goods.

Everybody knows Romania either because of Dracula and the land of the vampires, or because of Ceausescu and the land of communism. I'm afraid I'm about to disappoint you here, dear reader, but Dracula didn't influence me at all. The communist regime did. We were so controlled: everything we ate, how much we ate, what material possessions we had and how we dressed. The fear was present like a human being, not an emotion.

Electricity was cut off, after 6 p.m., almost daily. I studied by candlelight during my primary school years. TV consisted of only one channel, with Ceausescu and Congress aired every day. We were treated to cartoons on Saturdays and Sundays for one hour. We might have been gifted with movies, but I do not remember seeing any until the age of eight. In 1989 the Romanians got tired of being controlled and started a Revolution. The people won. However, for a young child, it meant a time of confusion, and even more fear and disillusionment.

Coming from a family of seven members, physical hard work was a way of life, not just an activity. It started at a very early age, too, from around ten years old, when the land was given back to the people. My father regained his family's land and started a small farm. The centre of our universe were our cows. My siblings and I had to tend to them in the fields from morning until evening, rain or shine.

But I loved it, because my father's land was next to the city's river. There I taught myself how to swim and catch fish. On that field I learnt how to start a fire and improvised making a stove from old materials found on the field. My siblings and I learnt how to choose mushrooms, prepare and eat them. Sometimes, we even went and stole corn from the cornfield, or sunflowers.

I hated waking up in the morning and going to the field every single day, but I also loved it. Now, in hindsight, I wouldn't change a thing. Growing up like that, in those times and conditions, gave me the life skills, values and principles that would guide me throughout my entire life. Communism taught me how to appreciate the food, water, clothes and shelter. The post-Revolution years taught me how to fight for myself, defend myself and distinguish the difference between the good and the bad.

My confidence was very low and my self-esteem almost non-existent; I felt inferior to other people, no matter how hard I worked. Our parents instilled in us the desire to study, so we could escape "the poor legacy" and build better lives for ourselves. It was during my primary school years that I learnt about England and fell in love with the language and the country. Since that time, I knew one day I would live in the UK. I didn't know when or how, but I knew it would be my reality, one day.

I'm telling you all these things because one day I did start to live my beautiful dream, and even when this beautiful dream almost turned into a nightmare, I discovered I had all the skills and the strong mindset to overcome everything that happened to me on a bright sunny day, in August 2014.

**Based on the wealth of knowledge, wisdom, and experience you have now, what would you like to say to yourself back then?**

*Dear Adina,*

*I am writing to you as your future self, at the ripe old age of thirty-eight. The reason for writing is to warn you and prepare you for what you are about to experience when you turn thirty-three. Nothing that you have lived so far in your breathtaking, beautiful Transylvanian city, Sebes, will compare with what is about to happen when you go on your usual, two-week holiday to visit your family.*

*You have always loved visiting your home town, meeting your friends and high school colleagues, laughing and enjoying the sweet memories of your childhood, especially the days you spent swimming in the river, while you were supposed to watch the cows.*

*On this late August day, I want you to know, you will wake up rejuvenated, eager to take your son and nephew to the park. You will go jogging and they will bike. You will feel so alive, happy and content with your life. You are so proud of yourself for making a very good living in London. You have your own business as a life coach and you trained as a Reiki master. You feel the world is your oyster and you plan to go on training as a counsellor, too. You love life and life loves you.*

*But this is about to change. On the walk to the park you will experience something that will change your life, but not in a good way. It won't happen immediately. It will start with one scary episode, followed by another and then another, each getting harder and harder to keep under control. Your heart will start racing at 2000km/h, your palms will be sweaty and you will feel drops of sweat falling down your forehead and spine. Your mind will race even faster than your heart. You will know instinctively there's something wrong with you. But what?*

*Then the visions will start. Looking back, they seem so surreal you will feel you are in a 3D cartoon horror. You can see your hands turning into an animal's claw. You know it's not real, but God, it feels real.*

*You will feel your soul coming out of your body at one point and climbing on the bathroom walls. "God," you say, "if I'm about to die, why does it have to be in the toilet?"*

*How funny you are, even in the last moment. Yes, it will feel like life is about to end, as the confusion and palpitations will be out of control. A thought will run through your head in this moment: "I love you God. I have to call Kate."*

*With fear in your heart, you will know your son is sleeping in his bedroom next door and could wake at any moment. You hear your inner voice shout: "I don't want him to see me like this. He'll be so scared. I have to call Kate. Where's Kate? She'll take care of my son. She'll take care of me. I'm losing my mind. What's going on?"*

You will understand the power of friendship in this moment as, bless Kate, she will arrive in five minutes. When she sees you, she will call an ambulance straight away. Even though you will be so scared, brace yourself, Adina, because unfortunately they will find nothing. They won't even take you to hospital. I hate to tell you, sweet Adina, that you will have to go through these episodes three evenings in a row, before finally they work out what's wrong. On the third evening, the doctors that visit will ask Kate if anything unusual has happened to you recently, and she will have the inspiration to say: "Oh, she was bitten by a dog while on holiday in her home country, Romania."

*The moment she utters those words you will be rushed to hospital. They will check your wound, which is bound so tightly. It will be purple; a deep, dark purple that never looks good. Lots of doctors will examine the wound, take your blood pressure, blood samples, put you in for a heart scan, eye examination, everything they can think of.*

I want to reassure you, Adina, that your free spirit, your stubbornness in the face of any hardship will be your secret weapon with which you will start to use to fight for your life.

*They will leave you alone, on your hospital bed, looking at the ceiling, painted in the same colour as the walls. It wasn't white. It will be a kind of a crème. It's so strange how your mind will start to think the weirdest thoughts. "Why do all UK hospitals look so weird?" You never noticed that before, so why notice that now? In hindsight, know that this is your own defence mechanism trying to distract you from the persistent, acute feeling something really bad is about to happen.*

*You won't know how long you will just lie on that bed, looking up at the ceiling, following the cracks that snake across it, wondering if your little boy will wake up. You will feel safe knowing Kate remained at home. She'll know how to comfort him, if he needs it.*

*Now I want you to brace yourself, Adina, and quieten your mind. Now's the time to remember all the moments when you had to protect yourself from danger and get ready, because any second now your little room is going to be filled to overflowing with doctors, and the words they say will shock you, but I want you to know you will be okay.*

*"Ms Oltean, you might have only ten days to live. We suspect you have rabies."*

*You will look at each of them in disbelief and start laughing: "I cannot die. I have a son to raise. What's rabies, anyway?" You won't stay to hear the answer.*

*You will stand up, take your clothes and leave. Thinking back, you won't remember if they tried to stop you; you won't remember if they said anything to you at all. All you will remember from that night is, following that statement, you decided you were going to completely change your life, stay by your son's bedside and look after him.*

*The next day, when the hospital calls to inform you that you have to go back in for more checks, you will refuse. Instead, you will get dressed and go to work. You refuse to stop your life and just wait to die.*

*After three more days they will call again. They will be concerned, so this time you will go, signing paperwork and receiving ten injection shots. Leaving the hospital armed with a checklist, you will remember you have to be aware if you become afraid of water. This will sound strange, and you won't know why this is important, so you won't ask; you will just go back to work for money to feed you and your son.*

*Ten days will pass, and although you will still have the panic attacks, you will know you aren't dying. Sadness will start to kick in. Why did they say I was about to die? What if I am still dying? What will happen to my son? You will start to feel that if it weren't for him, you wouldn't have to worry so much, you could just die in peace. Fifteen days will pass, and you will start to take comfort when you don't appear to be dying.*

*Adina, I want you to remember that when you had your son, your father died. To face the pain, to be strong for your new-born son, you closed down all your emotions. Adina, those emotions you know are caused by post-natal depression are going to start resurfacing now, and you will start to question your life and feel suicidal.*

*Every day you will ask yourself: "Why didn't I die? Do I have to act on this myself? Maybe, this is what everybody expects me to do? Yes, I think this is what I have to do. I have to kill myself. Hmmm, but how? I never thought of that. I think the easiest and fastest, and surest, is if I jump under a train. I wonder how many people will be upset with me for delaying their commute? Who cares! I was supposed to die twenty days ago, and I'm not dying."*

*Soon, you will feel the urge to tell someone what is going on. One month will go by and you know will you are not dying, but have the urge instead to kill yourself. Whose voice is it telling you that you should jump under a train? You will know it is not your voice.*

*Adina, when in the underground, put your hand on the wall and don't move until the Tube train has stopped and, when you are outside, call Dana. Tell her everything, even though you know she will tell you off for hiding it from her.*

*When you call your big sister, you will burst into tears and pour your heart out to her: "The doctors said I might die in ten days, but I'm not dying and it is more than a month now. Something to do with the dog bite, I don't know. But now I don't like my son, and I have this voice telling me I should jump under the train, but I don't want to."*

*She will calm you down enough and urge you to call Mom and, when you hear that familiar voice at the end of the phone, your words will tumble out in a hurried mess: "Mom, I need you. I'm depressed. I'm suicidal, I don't want to be here, but I am. My hair is falling out. My nails are blue, I'm sweating, and I have hallucinations. They don't last long, but I'm very scared. I need you to come. Now."*

*Your Mom will fly in immediately. After being with you for a week, you and your mom decide now's the time to call the priest. You feel you have to be ready for anything. You will assess your life, have no regrets, apart from the thought of not seeing your son grow up. But if you die, it wouldn't matter anyway.*

*When you see the priest, you will feel at peace, ready to go when the time is right. I want to tell you, my brave Adina, his feeling of being ready to die will not last long as, one day, you will wake up, look around the room and say: "Enough with this drama, with dying, with suicide, guilt and anger. I am better than this. I am strong. I am a warrior."*

*Adina, this is the day life prepared you for. All the pain, hardships, events in your life led you to this moment. This is the day you battle for your future. The battle of your life begins now.*

*You've been through two divorces, raised your son by yourself for six years now in a foreign country. You've built a successful business in Romania. You closed contracts, negotiated with big retailers in the UK. You know what you need. You need to remember your joy for life, to remember how to laugh again from your heart.*

*I want to remind you of the little Ho'oponopono prayer you used to love saying every day. This is the prayer that will bring the smile to your face again, because the truth is this will help you start your forgiveness process. You will forgive yourself for all the pain you had to go through.*

*Every day you will write: "I'm sorry I have these suicidal thoughts which I know are not mine. Please forgive me, my beautiful mind, for allowing these thoughts to disturb and scare you. I love you, my divine soul, for staying pure, kind and full of love. Thank you, Adina, for being strong, courageous and choosing life."*

*The next year you will spend meditating, training as a counsellor, and taking each day at a time. You will make it your mission to find at least three things you love during the day; a flower, a cloud, an unknown face in the bus, the colour of a stranger's eyes. And you will laugh at jokes, at movies, at your son's silly moments. And you will be living fully in each moment.*

*Adina, what happened to you was not your fault. It was a blessing in disguise. You had to go through this so your soul could grow. You needed the push because you were just floating through life despite being destined for greatness. You had to learn how to stay true to yourself, allow yourself to be vulnerable, ask for help. You had to apply the techniques and exercises you learnt on yourself, so you can confidently incorporate them in your business.*

*Adina, I want to reassure you God didn't punish you. God is love, and you are part of God. You are part of the love of the universe. You have a mission to help people. You know that.*

*It is your destiny.*

*If you didn't go through everything you went through, you wouldn't have appreciated what you have. Life is a contrast; you need both the good and the bad experiences. How can you be appreciative of the good if you've never experienced the bad? Life would be so dull otherwise.*

*The last thing I want to tell you is that I love you with all my heart, and I thank you for always following your heart.*

*Your most ardent supporter,*

*Adina*

**What golden nuggets did you learn from this experience?**
This whole experience was a healing process. Although it still feels like it was the darkest moment of my life, without it I wouldn't have found my identity, discovered who I really am. I would have

still been hiding behind my fears and limitations, imposed or self-imposed, denying my soul's purpose: to be happy and at peace with myself.

This episode made me realise who is truly important in my life: me.

I dedicated my life to pleasing others because I wanted to be liked and wanted. I wanted to belong somewhere. I understood that when I like myself, I want my own company, I feel like I belong anywhere life takes me.

I learnt the hard way to live in the moment. I learnt the hard way we cannot escape nor deny our inner child. If she needs healing, she will force you to heal, sooner or later. Only then will you find your true inner happiness and balance.

**What would you tell other women who might be experiencing this?**
If you feel that something is not quite right with you, seek help. Do not suppress your tears, your anger, your pain or despair. Unleash it fully without being afraid. Post-Natal Depression (PND) is not your fault. It's not something you consciously asked for, that you wanted in your life. It is there to show you that you have something to heal, from the past or the present. Regardless of what it is, do not ignore it, do not resist it. It will stay with you until you are strong enough to face it, and then it will hit you so hard that you will fall flat on your face. But I want you to know you can rise up stronger than ever before. Trust your soul; it knows what to do.

**What are some of the things you would have changed in this situation if you could?**

I wouldn't change anything. I would only learn more about the PND instead. I would ask myself more questions around the fact I couldn't cry for my father's death, and I couldn't cry when my son went through his horrible surgery. I would challenge those around me who considered me a strong person, asking why crying made me weak. I wish I knew this beast called PND can stay hidden in the shadow of our thoughts for a very long time, and it can attack you when you least expect it, just to remind you life is fragile and it's worth cherishing every single second of it.

**Any final words?**

Always remember you do the best you can with the best knowledge and resources you have. Later regrets are useless. Continuous learning is paramount.

**How can people get in touch with you?**

- Website: *www.thecgcentre.com*
- Facebook: *https://www.facebook.com/theconsciousnessandguidancecentre/*

"You are enough, I know sometimes it can be hard to see that, and you may be told differently by others, remember, you do not need people around you that are negative/toxic or make you feel less than you deserve. Put yourself at the top of the importance pile, you and the people you love deserve the best of you, not the rest of you."

– Lisa King –

# Trust in You, You've Got This

## Lisa King

*Inspirational speaker, author and mentor, creator of programmes, courses and workshops that empower and guide people to reach their highest potential, fulfil their brilliance and live life on their terms*

**W**hat are you passionate about and how are you contributing to the world?

With over twenty-five years in the health and fitness industry, and after training thousands of people to be physically, mentally and emotionally the best version of themselves, the biggest reward for me, still, is to see the amazing transformations achieved. I love seeing the changes that occur and the inspiration this brings to those around them, which then leads to greater health, peace, respect, love and understanding. My vision is to see millions of people with inner self-love, creating a happier, healthier, more peaceful world of acceptance, love and kindness, with inspiration and empowerment as the guiding force for generations to come.

**Describe a pivotal moment in your life you would like to share.**

I couldn't choose only one pivotal moment that highlighted the lack of self-love and self-respect I had, so I chose to share the ones that were life-changing for me in so many ways. These have acted like a snowball for me, and have played such a huge part in my life, growing and growing until it took a tragedy to explode it, shaping who I am today.

The first pivotal moment occurred continuously over a thirteen-year period, starting when I was two. It was the physical and mental abuse suffered by my mum at the hands of my dad and the many years of sleepless nights and torment we all suffered. The long-term effects of this not only led me to make many mistakes and bad choices throughout my life, but also gave me the strength, resilience and drive I have today.

The next pivotal moment, and one of the events in my life I buried so deeply, happened at the age of twelve. I was raped by two young men I knew, which led to me shutting down in so many ways. My lack of self-respect and self-worth at that time was so evident looking back, and the impact this had on my relationships was only to be truly discovered later in my life, as the masks I wore fitted so perfectly that nobody knew, even me.

Two major health scares followed, one at the age of seventeen, when I almost died from a burst appendix. This highlighted two things to me. The first was that, even after having a seriously close shave with death, my dad still couldn't step up and be there. That hurt, really bad, and was proof yet again that nothing would come between him and the life he wanted. For me, I still questioned what needs to happen for him to just be Dad. The second was that I should've got this checked a lot earlier; it was an indicator to me of how much physical pain I could endure, but also the importance of recognising I needed help and needed to put me first, not just put up with it.

The second health scare came three years later. After playing football, I was in significant pain, with tingling and numbness down my legs. After a hospital visit and subsequent tests, it was revealed that I had two breaks in my lumbar spine and needed urgent surgery to fuse my spine, as it was distended into my spinal cord and needed to be stabilised quickly. I had a week before the surgery to get things organised, and I got to play what could have been my final game of football. I scored a hat-trick, but how stupid was I?

A pivotal moment happened several years later, and this loss of connection was one of the most obvious choices I have had to make, yet one of the hardest. After almost twenty years of friendships, connection and competitive sport, I was faced with the realisation I had no choice but to retire from playing my beloved football, as another back surgery was suggested. This paled into insignificance at the time though, as my partner Becky was diagnosed with cervical cancer and had to face intense chemotherapy and radiotherapy over the next five months. The tragedy is that, less than a year later, she committed suicide. Over the next couple of years my health declined massively, leading to my subsequent breakdown, gradual road to recovery and the inspiration to help others.

**Looking back, what made it such an important part of your life journey?**
Each pivotal moment played such a huge part in the direction of my life. Each highlighted the lack of self-love and self-respect I had for

myself, why I behaved the way I did, felt the way I felt and wore the masks I wore. The accumulation of events in my life snowballed into a giant boulder that had to come crashing into something at some time. It took the tragedy of Becky dying and my subsequent breakdown for me to be at the lowest point in my life, for me to realise I needed to step through these events and find Lisa again; the Lisa without the masks. Looking back on my journey, I didn't have an enormous amount of compassion for myself. Now, I am the most peaceful, happy and loving Lisa I have ever been. I have beautiful relationships with those around me, I say no when I want to, yes when I want to and I feel amazing being able to do that with no negative emotions attached. I guide others to find their inner self-love, to be the best version of themselves, inspiring others around them to do the same. That, to me, is priceless.

**Based on the wealth of knowledge, wisdom and experience you have now, what would you like to say to yourself back then?**

*Sitting on the stairs in your pyjamas, I can see you curled up, head between your legs, trying not to breathe too loudly so nobody can hear you. Your breathing is shallow, breathing into your lap, so as not to be heard. You had been asleep until the door opened, and everything started again. It was the noise you dreaded most days.*

*I know, right now, everything feels so scary. You don't know what to do. You wish you were strong enough to stop him. You feel lost, sad, angry and lonely. It will stop soon, your mum will be okay. Steve is asleep, at least you hope he is, and you can sleep again soon. Until the next noise, or the next raised voice wakes you, as it always does.*

*I am here for you. You are a beautiful little angel who needs to sleep. You are so tired. It is not your job to look after everyone. I know you are exhausted, and you just want to protect your mum and Steve. I'm here to hold you, protect you and keep you safe, and I will never leave your side. I know you are scared that if you sleep, something bad will happen to your mum but, let me tell you, your mum will be okay. You will all be okay. You will always have your mum's unconditional love; she will be there through everything. You will have some testing times over the years to come, and she will be there for you with her compassion and her love through all of it, standing by your side.*

*I know it feels like it's your fault when he doesn't show up. Why doesn't he love you? Why can't he just be there for once? What have you done wrong? You will question yourself and feel completely unloved. He will let you down so many times through your life. Your dad does love you, he just feels it's okay because that's what happened to him. He thinks he's okay, so you'll be okay too. But the truth is, he's not okay, he's far from okay, but that doesn't make you feel any better right now, I know.*

*To everyone else he is so generous and funny. He'll do anything for his mates; what a legend, a nice bloke. To you, he is supposed to be Dad, to protect you, love you, keep you safe, not the one creating your sadness. He is supposed to be the one you turn to if you need a hug, which only comes if he has nothing better to do. Lisa, it isn't supposed to be like that.*

*The violence will start when your mum is pregnant with Steve. You were two and, over the next thirteen years, he will leave several times for weeks on end, without a call or a care, have multiple affairs and, worst of all, he will hurt your mum, in so many ways. She will be knocked unconscious, beaten, verbally abused, emotionally abused. You will hear most of it, see some of it, feel all of it. When you are around ten or eleven years old, he will call you a slag, and you will be spoken to like you don't matter because you tried to help your mum by shouting at him. There are too many things to write down, but I just want you to know none of what he says is true; you are beautiful, loved, worthy and more than good enough. His behaviour was his choice; it was not your fault he did what he did, it was all on him.*

*Lisa, you won't understand the significance of this day for many years, but you are going to be in the field behind the houses in a den with two boys you know well. Without knowing why, you are going to feel a little scared and unsure as to what's happening. You are only twelve and you've never been in this situation before. One of the boys is going to reassure you everything is going to be okay, while the other is not sure what is happening, but he will still go along with it.*

*You will find yourself lying there; you have your trousers off and one of the boys is kneeling between your legs, saying it's going to be okay. He will lie on top of you and put his penis inside you. He knows he shouldn't be doing it, and so does the other one.*

*At this point, you won't know how to feel; you will feel numb and confused and not sure what or why it is happening, or if it really matters. After, you will carry on your day as if nothing has happened, as if you have already blocked it out, but mentally you will have started to shut down.*

*When you are twelve or thirteen, your dad will leave again, choosing to have hardly any contact at all with you or Steve for a whole year. I know your heart will break and, with each time he comes back and goes again, your heart will break again and again. This is not how any of you should be treated, and certainly not children.*

*It's going to be tiring. You are going to feel like you can't talk to anybody, because it needs to be kept a secret. So, you will feel like you have two lives. At home you will constantly feel like you are walking on eggshells, not able to talk about it, confront him or to speak to your mum about it. Your mum will just keep going, like she's on autopilot. She works so hard and will do anything for you and Steve. She will keep going to support you, because your dad won't be around very much. Then you have the other life, the one where you wear the mask, the joker, the one who craves love and attention from your peers, who throws themselves into sports and plays to keep busy, the one who is making bad choices to fit in.*

*This is one of the many reasons you will feel you have to tackle the world alone, that you don't need anyone's help. You will feel like you can't trust anyone, because everyone you should have been able to trust wasn't there, so you'll have to do it yourself.*

*School is going to feel like your safe place for a while; you'll enjoy primary school, do really well, have fun, play, do all the things kids are supposed to do. You will sing and dance for your family, enjoy sports and excel in your handwriting. Things will change quite a lot when you get to secondary school, and life at home will be intense. As you get older, it's not okay to be struggling to sleep, constantly holding things in. But sport is going well, and that's your escape; your PE teacher thinks you have so much potential. You are going to be a sports champion and you are going to love the friendships and the sense of belonging it gives you.*

*In the next few years you will rebel. You will shoplift, and won't really care what will happen if you get caught. You will smoke and drink and, even though you are great at sports, you want to have that connection, and your friends smoke and drink. It's the start of things unravelling for you. School will become less important, your grades will start to slip, but you don't really care. Your dad is still beating your mum and you've had enough. He always said he would only leave if one of his kids told him to go. The time comes, so that's what you do. Unbeknown to you, your mum had reached the point where enough was enough too. She tells him it's time to go, on her terms, not his.*

*At age seventeen, you are lucky to be alive. You had been in hospital for three days. They didn't know what was wrong; things weren't adding up and they were unsure as to what was causing your pain. Then your appendix burst, and you were told you are very lucky to be alive. During your hospital stay, your dad still shows his true colours; you nearly died, and he still didn't bother.*

*This will upset you, but you will have so many other people there for you.*

*Over the next few years, you see your dad on and off, learning of two more children he has had, and you feel for them immediately. He then meets Ann and, in the process of emigrating to Australia when you are eighteen, he has to disown you to be able to gain entry to Australia. To be honest, it will feel like he disowned you many years ago.*

*You will start playing competitive football at nineteen, and be really good at it. You love the team, the connection, the banter, the friends. You will play for one year and then be told you have broken your back, in two places, and life is about to change. The doctor will tell you he doesn't think you'll play again, but you have other ideas, and give yourself one year out and you'll be back. That's a pretty adventurous timescale considering you are in a cast for three months, but you play after fifty-one weeks. Am I surprised? Of course not; it's you and you are one of the most determined people I know.*

*Relationships over the next few years will become a bit of a pattern. After coming out to your mum and Steve, you have many relationships with some beautiful women, who you love and have lots of fun with. The problem is the moment they get close to you, the emotions bring up the barriers, because you can't cope with feeling vulnerable. You can't trust them and let them in, and you walk away from each one, even though you truly do love some of them very much. This will continue well into your thirties.*

*You will have many relationships throughout your football life, but the significant one will be with Becky. You will know her for eleven years before having a relationship with her and, after four years, you are not sure whether she is the one for you. However, at the time of questioning the relationship, you both receive shocking news. Becky has a huge tumour, has cervical cancer; there is no way you will walk away from her now. This will rock both your worlds, but you are both strong. You talk, hold each other, and you vow to fight it with everything you both have. Becky will become very reliant on you, but you are so used to this feeling, it doesn't scare you. You will know you have the strength to be there for her. Unbeknown to Becky, not long after her diagnosis is the time your back flares up again, and you will need to stop playing your beloved football, which will break your heart. But you have something you need to deal with first that is far more important; you have to help Becky fight the cancer.*

*It will be five months of intense chemo and radiotherapy that takes its toll. Becky will struggle to sleep at times and you will stay awake, rubbing her head, holding her until she can sleep. You are her rock, her everything; you will give her the strength to get through this and you become so close again that you even get matching tattoos. Becky will start playing football again once she has the strength, but you won't be able to go to watch, as it's too hard to watch the same team you are now unable to play for.*

*Several months later, Becky will come home from football and you will have a conversation that will be life-changing. She knows something is wrong, and you know you need to speak to her, to* tell her how you are feeling. You have lost yourself somewhere along the way; you are unsure of your feelings, and having to stop playing football feels like your right arm has been taken away. With the uncertainty of your back, losing connection and being unsure of your feelings for Becky, you will feel so lost and know you need some space to sort it out.

It will be a really hard conversation because you do love Becky. She will struggle with what you are saying, to the point she will threaten to kill herself as she can't live without you, and you, being you, will do everything to ease her pain. So you agree a holiday is a good idea, that maybe this is what you both need after everything that has happened.

You will wake up the next morning, ready for your week. Becky will give you a hug before she goes to work that will be so intense. She will hold you like she has never held you, and she will tell you how much she loves you, looking at you with those beautiful blue eyes. She will say it again just before she walks out the door, and you will say it back to her. It is only a day later you realise the significance of what happened.

You know something is terribly wrong, but you can only inform the police that Becky is missing after twenty-four hours. Later that day they will knock on the door. You will be sat with two of your friends after being awake all night, ready to drive anywhere if you heard from her, and in the early hours you will have a violent rush of nausea come over you and you will cry uncontrollably. You will know it is Becky, you know something has happened, you just won't know what. As they walk in the front room, they will tell you her body has been found in the River Thames. Once they saw the tattoo on your wrist, they knew. Becky was gone.

The next two weeks will pass by in a haze. So many people around, drinking to forget, to the point that, some days, drink became breakfast. There is identifying Becky's body, funeral arrangements, going to see her before the funeral, trying to get some sleep, which does not go well either. Thankfully, you had discussed what Becky wanted for her funeral when she was diagnosed, so that was one less pressure.

Lisa, the first nine months will pass by with too much alcohol, you will work all the hours you can and, at the weekends, you will get drunk and take drugs. You will stumble from one mistake to another, getting involved with people you shouldn't while spending days wondering what is going on and how you can deal with it. You will start to eventually feel better – and then the inquest date arrives.

You will be put on the stand at Becky's inquest, to relive every moment again, like you hadn't already. You had been doing okay, until you were in court on the stand, being questioned about Becky's death. It will be so tough, but you are tougher.

The following year, life takes another unexpected turn, this time for the better. After the inquest, you have some closure, and life can return to some form of normality, although, how can life be normal again? While you are still taking the drugs and drinking, *you will meet Penny, and she will give you a reason to get your act together. You stop taking the drugs immediately. After all, you didn't need the drugs; you wanted the drugs, to feel that connection, but you can have the connection without the drugs. You get on, have lots of laughter, and she will be a straightforward, no-nonsense woman who can see beyond your masks. You can be happy again, feel safe and loved. You will start to rebuild your life, to step away from the people who are not enhancing your life, to learn, understand your masks and why they are there. You step through the emotions that held you back for so long and get the help you need to finally deal with your constant health issues, putting you first. You will inspire so many people around you with your honesty, strength, courage and passion.*

*And this is when the next chapter in your life truly begins.*

**What golden nuggets did you learn from this experience?**
I know I was looking externally for the love I needed and wanted. I now know the love I needed meant I had to look inside to find the love for myself. Having no self-love or respect for myself led me to make some bad choices, to not care about what happened to me, to shut off my emotions to others and put myself at the bottom of every pile of importance. I also learnt I was not responsible for other people's actions, regardless of what they say or do.

The journey of finding Lisa again, with the added strength and courage I have received from these experiences, has been exhilarating. I have stepped through some very deep emotions, which has been hard but so very worth it. I now know my purpose was to step through all of these experiences, to have a wealth of knowledge so that I can guide others to live the life they deserve, to have inner peace, self-love, happiness, and to then inspire and guide generations to come on how to have that same inner love.

Once I had trust and love for myself, I would never feel abandoned or alone again, because I have ME.

**What would you tell other women who might be experiencing this?**
You are enough. I know sometimes it can be hard to see that, and you may be told differently by others, but remember, you do not need people around you that are negative/toxic or make you feel less than you deserve. Put yourself at the top of the importance pile. You and the people you love deserve the best of you, not the rest of you.

Take time out to find you again, do things that make you happy. Talk to people you can trust, say no to things you do not want to do, to create time and energy to do the things you do want to do. You deserve the very best.

**What are some of the things you would have changed about the situation if you could?**
This is by far the hardest question to answer. Of course, I wouldn't want my mum to suffer the way she did, for Becky to have died, for my brother and I to have had to endure the constant neglect from our dad or to have my innocence taken from me at twelve. Of course not. The question is, would I have made the changes if these things

hadn't snowballed and then crashed, leading to my breakdown, to losing my best friend? That was the moment I knew things had to change, when I couldn't get any lower. Would anything else have put me there? I'm not sure it would. So, my heart says one thing and my head says another. Is there really an easy answer to this question? Of course not. I am who I am today because of my life experiences. It is what it is.

**Any final words?**

Having self-love, knowing, loving and accepting you, all of you, is the most powerful experience of your life. No longer feeling you need to find/have external love to feel whole is beautiful. You are already whole, everything else is a beautiful bonus.

**How can people get in touch with you?**

- Email: *isaking@stepupstandtall.com*
- Facebook: *www.facebook.com/stepupstandtall*

"I learned that I am the director and star of the movie of my life and that by changing the way I think, asking myself how I want to feel and what I need now, that I can create my own reality. If I am not liking what I am seeing I need to look within and be the change I want to see."

– Lavinia Sanders –

# The Power of Balance

## Lavinia Sanders

*International award-winning motivational speaker,
Energy Balancing trainer, Reiki master and Clarity creator*

What are you passionate about and how are you contributing to the world?

I am passionate about empowering women to reconnect with themselves, step up and take responsibility for creating their own life and happiness. I believe we are all connected and unique, with our own set of talents and gifts, and it is our duty to share them with the world. I work with women to help them identify personal triggers that throw them off balance, and to understand the true power of their thoughts, emotions and actions (TEA). I believe we all have the power within us to restore harmony and balance and to create the life we deserve.

My company, Balance with Lavinia, provides free resources to help women to create more balance in all areas of their life and fully accredited, certified workshops, retreats, and online programmes. It is my belief that, if each person takes responsibility for their own happiness and well-being, the world would be a much better place full of lots more happy and balanced people.

**Describe a pivotal moment in your life that you would like to share.**
The 7th of September 2015, I received a parcel from New York.
I love to receive parcels through the post. It reminds me of being a
child at Christmas, and the excitement of opening up your presents
with the anticipation of what will be inside. On this occasion, the
parcel contained a beautiful china cup and saucer from an old friend
from Dublin who was now living in New York. With it came a note:
"back home in Ireland a nice cup of tea can help any situation so
I'm sending you this cup and saucer for your nice cup of tea". The
situation in question was my recent diagnosis of breast cancer and
my imminent treatment plan.

Rewind eight weeks, and I had a phone call that would change my
life for the better, although at the time I thought I had entered a
living hell. On Monday 13th of July, 2015, (a date etched into my
memory), I got a call to go back to the hospital for a biopsy after a
routine mammogram. It was a Monday and I was in Glastonbury,
having just completed a wonderful five days of Reiki master training.
The hospital wanted me to go in that day, but I was 180 miles away.
The journey home from Glastonbury was a bit of a blur. There
were lots of stops to just cry and cry. The ten days that followed
were the longest ten days of my life. If I had been nominated for
an Oscar during those ten days, I reckon I would have had a very
good chance of winning it. Outwardly, I continued on as if life was
normal; I didn't tell many people, just my immediate family. I got up
every day and put a smile on my face, and continued to say yes to
people even though all I wanted to do was go to my bed and cry and
cry. Inwardly, I was so scared, and in complete denial and disbelief.
I was terrified of not being around for my daughters, who were aged

seventeen and thirteen. Who would be there to support them for all the milestones in their lives? I didn't want to leave my husband; we had plans of more travel and adventures together. I didn't want him to be alone to bring up our two beautiful daughters.

When the results came back, I received the news I had been dreading. The consultant, Dr Delilah Hassanally (a wonderful compassionate surgeon), said to me I have good news and bad news! The bad news was I did have breast cancer. The good news was they had caught it very early. Speed was of the essence. I needed to get booked into hospital to get it chopped out as soon as possible. Even then, sitting in the consultation room, I remember saying to the consultant: "I'm going on holiday to France in eight days' time." What was I thinking?

The week that followed the diagnosis was full of scans – CT, MRI, blood tests, but again, to the outside world, I was continuing life as normal. I was trying my best not to show any sign of the devastation, fear and anxiety I was feeling. I had surgery six days later and went to the south of France nine days after. I didn't want to let anyone down and cancel our holiday. My thinking was I might as well be in France for my recovery as at home in UK, plus we had guests coming to stay with us. The reason this is a pivotal moment in my life is because it helped me see that for most of my life, which has been very privileged, I put everyone else and their needs before myself. Now I know this is a good thing to do, to be kind and think of others, but not if it is to the detriment of yourself. I realised this was something that started a long time before my cancer diagnosis and, indeed, we would have to go back to an incident in my childhood when I was six years old for the conscious beginning of a need to please people, and of the critic that would sit on my shoulder for more than forty years.

**Looking back, what made it an important part of your journey?**
Getting diagnosed with breast cancer really brought home to me the importance of being present in the moment. I remember one of the most difficult parts of my cancer journey was the six days of waiting to hear if I had cancer or not. During that time, I kept saying to myself: "If I have breast cancer, I am going to ... " And, interestingly, it wasn't to go off on a five-star holiday, to go out shopping, climb a mountain; it was the simple things like spend more time with my family and friends, not work as hard, not worry so much about what other people think, to have more fun, to make each day count. Getting cancer was like a gift from the universe. But it is only a gift if you make friends with it and see what it is you are supposed to learn from the experience. It really made me look at my life and what is truly important to me. I realised no amount of material possessions – and I should add at this point I had a bit of a thing for shoes and handbags – are going to make you happy. Ultimately, if you are faced with a life-threatening situation, it's not your Louboutins or your Chanel handbag that will get you through, it is the connections you have with yourself and those around you. Every day is a gift, and it is up to you to make it count.

Based on the wealth of knowledge, wisdom and experience you have now, what would you like to say to yourself back then?

*My Dearest Darling Beautiful Lavinia,*

*In a few moments you are going to experience an incident that will have a profound effect on your life. A little part of you will die; the innocent, non-judgemental way you look at the world and people. It will be more than forty years before you regain this part of yourself, before you will banish the critic that will sit on your shoulder after the incident that is about to happen. This critic will remain invisible and will drive you to achieve lots of great things in your life but, ultimately, it will be part of the reason you hit rock-bottom, get diagnosed with breast cancer and enter a phase of your life that can only be described as a living hell.*

*So, before we talk about the incident, let me tell you up to this point in your life you have been loved, nurtured and encouraged to shine your light. You especially love to dance, and this is something that will bring you joy throughout your life. You feel very connected to your family. You have a very close relationship with your parents, your little sister Maria, your grandparents, aunts, uncles and cousins. You have experienced the joy that comes from being part of a loving family. You have been surrounded by a deep, anchoring love, lots of laughter, singing and dancing. You will never lose this lovely connection, and it will be a driver, propelling you in your ultimate life purpose to help people connect with themselves and others.*

*Despite the sadness and humiliation you are about to endure, you will become aware for the first time you have an inner desire for fairness and balance, and you have the courage to stand up to injustice. So, let's go back to that time at school when you were six years old. "Hayes, get up here to the front of the class immediately," your teacher will roar. You will be terrified, will have no idea what you have done wrong. "So, little madam, everyone thinks you are very clever. Well, you are clearly not as clever as everyone thinks you are!" You will be made to stand in front of your new class and say out loud, "I am not as clever as everyone thinks I am." Lavinia, I want you to know that everything is going to be okay, and you have done nothing wrong. You are so embarrassed, and some of your classmates are laughing at you. Your 'crime' was to write in pencil (a red pencil from your beautiful new pencil case in the shape of Spain, that you got on your recent holiday), instead of writing in ink pen. Something will happen in that moment that will also start a behaviour that will continue throughout your life.; you will not allow your new classmates or your new teacher to see how upset you are. You will keep that inside you.*

*You will grieve in private at different times in your life, like the time when you lost your second baby. You will be standing on the platform with all the other early morning commuters on your way to London. Your beautiful, precious second baby will leave your body, there on that platform. You will not make a scene; you will just stand there in a pool of blood as the other people board the train. You will very calmly call your husband to come and get you. You will be brave, but you will cry and cry in private. But nothing will prepare you for when you lose your hero and mentor, your* dad. Before he leaves this world, he will teach you lots: how to work hard, how to be kind and caring, how to laugh, how to love and be loved. He was a great man and had lots of sayings that will stay with you forever, like: "It's nice to be nice" and "always treat everyone with kindness and respect."

But, as you stand in front of your classmates reciting "I am not as good as everyone thinks I am," you are becoming aware of the power of words and the negative effect they can have on people. The words you were made to say out loud will stick in your subconscious for a long time, and you will have a burning desire to always prove yourself to those around you. People's approval will become very important. That critic on your shoulder will spend many years telling you that you are not good enough. My gorgeous innocent girl, you are good enough, more than good enough.

A couple of weeks earlier, you moved into your new house, and this is your new school. Unfortunately, the school didn't have room in your year group, so they put you in a class a year ahead. This will be the first time in your life you can remember feeling out of your depth. You will have lots of things to deal with – you are two years younger than some of your classmates, and your teacher is not happy having an extra child in her class. You are clever and you will cope with the academic work, but you will struggle on an emotional level at the beginning.

I want you to know your beautiful personality will really start to show some of the wonderful qualities you have inside you. You are very brave and fearless at times. Over the next couple of weeks, your teacher will make your life hell, pointing out every little thing you do wrong. You will desperately try to fit in with your classmates and make new friends and try to anticipate your teacher's next move. It will be exhausting. It will all come to a head when your teacher asks you to read out loud a piece from a book you've never seen before. You will stumble with the words on the page in front of you. She will scream at you. She screams all the time, but you will be very brave. She will make you stand at the front of the class again, hold out your hand and she will hit you over your knuckles with a large wooden ruler. She will draw blood. You will run out of the school and all the way home to your mum. Your mum will be horrified, but very calm. She will clean up your hand and take you back to the school. She will be walking very fast and you will have to run to keep up. You are worried about what is going to happen; will you get into more trouble? Your mum will make a formal complaint about the teacher. It turns out this is not the first complaint about this teacher. You will go back home with your mum and feel safe, secure and happy. When you go back to school, there is a new teacher who is kind and smiley.

My beautiful girl, what you are not aware of right now is that this incident will trigger behaviour in you that will serve you well for most of your life but will also contribute to you hitting rock-bottom and getting very sick. You have always been a good girl, but after this incident you will always try to please everyone, make sure your teachers like you and that you are friends with everyone. You will always try to anticipate situations in class, especially regarding reading out loud. At times it will be exhausting, but you will cope. It will be a long time before you feel comfortable *reading out loud in front of people, but you will. You will always be worried about other people and how they feel, always trying to make sure everyone is okay.*

*You have so much to look forward to, dear precious girl. You are popular at school and have loads of friends. You make friends easily and with all the different groups, as you don't want anyone to feel left out. You are very competitive and do well in everything. You win prizes for your dancing and basketball. That critic sitting on your shoulder will start to set the bar very high as you think this is what people expect from you. This will be good at times and propel you forward in life, but it will also be very stressful, and you will be disappointed with yourself too. I want to tell you that you are always good enough just as you are. You don't need other people's approval. People like you because you are kind, caring and fun to be around.*

*Lavinia, you have no idea how blessed you are to have the strong family foundations your parents have given you. These foundations will be strengthened with the arrival of your little brother, Brian, and baby sister Andrea. They will be the pillars that hold you up when times get difficult, like when your first serious relationship breaks up. Your family will do what they do best, by surrounding you with love and support.*

*The heartache you will feel from the break-up will pass, and you will go on to meet the most special person you have ever met; your husband, best friend and soulmate, Graeme. He will teach you so much about being yourself and enjoying life. He is kind, brilliant, caring, tall and handsome. He will teach you the importance of having balance in your life. Although you come from completely different backgrounds – he grew up in Africa, you grew up in Dublin – he too has been fortunate to have the grounding and security of a very strong family background. You will be fortunate enough to travel the world for work and pleasure. This will prove difficult at times as you will move far away from your family. A particularly difficult time will be your first Christmas away from your family, when you move to Singapore for work. Despite sitting in a beautiful beach resort in Thailand on Christmas Day with Graeme and your friends, you will be wishing you were back home in Dublin with your family. You will be missing all the things you have taken for granted over the years: popping into aunty Clare and uncle Vinny's house before lunch, the discussion over who was doing the washing-up, Mum cooking the best Christmas lunch, being made to eat at least two Brussels sprouts, Dad falling asleep in his chair after lunch. But, like everything else in life, Lavinia, you will handle it.*

*By far the best thing that will happen in your life with Graeme will be the birth of your two beautiful daughters, Jordan and Lauren. You will never have experienced so much love and joy. They will continue to bring you joy, laughter and happiness throughout your life. You share the bringing up of the girls together, and Graeme will be a very hands-on dad. One of the best compliments you will receive will come from your mum. She will be talking to her friend and she will say, "Lavinia really enjoys her children and loves being around them." This is so true. You cherish all the time you spend with the girls. At times, you will struggle to get the balance of working and being a mum right.*

*You will decide to give up your corporate career and run your own business, which will give you a lot more freedom to be with your girls, and be around the gorgeous home you will build with Graeme. The holistic business you start will grow and become very successful, with lots of regular, lovely clients. You will always feel the need to give back to society, as you feel very blessed. You will do lots of charity work that you will enjoy. You will particularly like working with the charity Homestart. Homestart helps families with children under the age of five who are struggling, be that financially, emotionally, through lack of parental guidance or lack of support. You will feel, because you have been so supported by your family, that you want to give back. You will love this work. You will do a huge amount of work with ladies who have been diagnosed with breast cancer. You will discover you are very good at holding a safe space, and you are empathetic and compassionate. These women will be on an emotional roller coaster, feeling shocked, angry, sad, stressed, anxious, confused and tired. You will provide different tools and relaxation strategies that will really help the ladies during their treatment.*

*You can see, and your clients will confirm, the benefits of the work you will do. Like with everything, you will strive to be the best and will complete many training courses to allow you to better serve your clients with chronic pain, cancer and palliative care. However, dear gorgeous girl, on the 13th of July, 2015, at the age of forty-eight, you will get a phone call that will cause the world you have built for yourself and your family to tumble down. It will completely challenge the pillars of strength you thought were supporting you, but it will also be one of the best gifts you have been given in life!*

**What golden nuggets did you learn from this experience?**

I learnt the peace, calm and bliss that comes with living in the present. I learnt the power of my thoughts and emotions and the effect they have on my actions. I learnt I am director and star of the movie of my life, and that by changing the way I think, asking myself how I want to feel and what I need now, I can create my own reality. If I am not liking what I am seeing, I need to look within and be the change I want to see.

But the most important thing I learnt from this experience is to get out of my head, connect with my heart, surround myself with people that lift my energy, have fun every day and, whatever life challenges me with, I will handle it. I take full responsibility now for my own happiness and life. I have rekindled the child-like curiosity and awareness, and I love that there are infinite possibilities available for each of us at all times.

**What would you tell other women who might be experiencing this?**

Take each day one at a time. Sometimes you might have to break that down to one hour at a time. Know you will get through it and handle it. Surround yourself with people who raise your energy, or join a group or community where you feel this and feel supported. Make peace with your cancer or the situation you find yourself in. Make it your friend, not your enemy. Ask yourself: what lesson is this situation here to teach me? What do I want and need right now? Give gratitude for the good in your life. Don't wait to do the things you want to do or say, that make you truly happy. This is it, folks. Don't delay, do it TODAY. Find some fun and joy in your life today.

**What are some of things you would change about the situation if you could?**

I would never go back and change things, as I believe who I am today is a combination of all my life experiences, good and bad, and I am very happy with who I am and where I am in my life. I believe in moving forward one step at a time. I understand now not to take things personally, not to neglect myself – my mind, body and soul – that everything changes, and situations will pass. I wish I had spent less time worrying about silly things, about trying to make things perfect.

I believe we cannot go back and change the past, but every day we wake up, we get to recreate the future, and that's exciting.

**Any final words?**

Life is for living today; be present, show up in all areas of your life as your authentic self. Always do your best and smile. Find the fun in the everyday things you have to do and appreciate all you have. Don't wait; take action today to live the life you want. Allow yourself to be happy, you deserve it.

**How can people get in touch with you?**
- Website: *www.balancewithlavinia.com*
- Facebook: *'Balance with Lavinia'*
- Instagram: *@balance_with_lavinia*
- LinkedIn: *'Lavinia (Hayes) Sanders'*

"Everyone is unique and chooses to deal with life experiences differently. What I learned is the more we can understand and manage our emotions living in the present, the more control and choice we have to make the right decisions."

– Kathryn Charlton –

# Your Inner Strength Allows You to Flourish

### Kathryn Charlton

*A motivational speaker, mentor, writer and transformational
coach who supports families and young people in discovering
their authentic selves*

What are you passionate about and how are you
contributing to the world?
For over eleven years, I have been working closely
with hundreds of young people, educating and caring for them to
develop the right tools, which will enable them to prosper and lead
fulfilling lives, right through to adulthood.

I am passionate about helping families to thrive in the highly
pressurised, materialistic society we live in. The more love and
support a child receives within a family, the more able they'll be to
grow into valued members of society.

My mission is to support as many families as possible, so they can
flourish and lead whole-hearted and compassionate lives. I have
created different resources to support families in achieving this.

**Describe a pivotal time in your life you wish to share.**

I knew from a very early age I wanted to live my life very differently to the way my parents chose. They had a very insular relationship, so I always felt like an outsider in my own home, which is why I was going to do things differently in my own marriage. However, the pendulum swung the other way. At the time I met my husband, I didn't know I needed to heal myself and learn new ways of being. If the truth be told, I married a version of my father, because I only knew a certain way of experiencing love, which wasn't healthy and didn't serve me.

This all changed when I completed the self-development course, Neuro-Linguistic Programming (NLP). It changed my life and empowered me to slowly start taking off my invisible armour to find the real me. I was picking up tools I could use in everyday life that enabled me to approach situations differently and interact with people on a different level. Life was no longer grey and lifeless, but vibrant and worth enjoying. I felt like I was transforming into a beautiful butterfly. I was also learning new ways to think, behave and love.

The other pivotal moment in my life was when I decided to go to Relate counselling on my own, even when my husband refused to go. The counsellor helped me to understand what made my relationship so toxic and unhealthy. By her explaining to me how a healthy relationship should be, it gave me the strength to know that ending my relationship was the best thing to do for everyone involved. It also helped me find the motivation and strength I so desperately needed to break away from the abusive relationship once and for all.

**Looking back, what made it such an important part of your life journey?**

Undertaking the NLP course gave me a new-found vitality for life which was intoxicating and spurred me on to continue my journey of self-development and self-discovery. It is an amazing journey; I have found the Buddhist teachings a great guiding light, and mindfulness an amazing gift for staying in the present and grounded. The path has given me the opportunity to meet some amazing people who have also inspired me and introduced me to new ways of thinking, as well as experiencing genuine loving and supportive relationships.

Without these learnings and experiences, I wouldn't be the person or parent I am proud to be today. Loving your children in a way that enables them to flourish isn't easy, especially when your role models haven't been able to show you how to do this. I don't always get it right, but now I have a number of tools I can call upon when reflecting on situations and what to do.

I now have a better understanding and references to what constitutes a healthy relationship – you don't have to earn love or try to be what someone else wants. Work on being the best version of yourself, and there will be someone out there who will love you just the way you are.

**Based on the wealth of knowledge, wisdom and experience you have now, what would you like to say to yourself back then?**

*Dearest darling Kathryn,*

*I know the notion of family will be really important to you when you grow up and something you will want to cherish more than anything. You will work really hard to provide your daughter with the loving, supportive family environment in which you want her to grow up; a different environment to your own childhood. However, there will be numerous occasions when you feel you have failed her.*

*The first will be on your first Mother's Day. You are not busy opening cards and enjoying family time – what you dream of doing – instead you will find yourself packing up yours and your daughter's belongings, ready to move out of Army married quarters because your husband has told you he doesn't want to be in the marriage any more. Your feeling of devastation will be incomprehensible. It will be like mourning a death; the death of a marriage you won't be given the opportunity to try to save or understand why it has failed. The sense of powerlessness is palatable. This day is meant to be so memorable, the first of many happy Mother's Day memories you want to create, but instead you will be packing your life into cardboard boxes. Once again you will adopt survival mode to help you get through it, which is what you learn to do in childhood.*

*So let's take a journey back, to where it all started, the day you were born. Your arrival is a greatly anticipated, momentous occasion. Your loving parents count down the days until you make your way into the world. Sadly, things don't go as planned. Once your mummy is taken to the local hospital, it is clear there are complications and both of you will be rushed to a larger hospital, where they are able to deal with your difficult birth. Although you arrive into the world safe and sound and mummy is physically okay, I want to let you know that a couple of weeks later, she will get very sick mentally and will be taken away from you. You will feel very alone without your mummy to snuggle up to, her familiar scent and to hear her soft, soothing tones which you've grown so used to in her tummy.*

*I will be there for you, to soothe and cherish you whenever you need to feel safe, secure and loved. Your daddy will do his best, giving you mummy's milk and caring for you in the only way he knows, however, you will miss the chance to bond with the person you know most, our wonderful mummy. The doctors advise your daddy he will always need to keep a close eye on our mummy and take great care of her, so she doesn't experience too much stress in her life. So you will learn, for the rest of your childhood, to be extremely well-behaved and, most importantly, to not cause any upset, so as to not stress your mummy.*

*This tense and anxious environment will be the start of your life and, although your childhood and early part of your adulthood will be about survival and just getting through each day, I promise you, those feelings will not last forever, and you will find another way.*

*The summer before your fifth birthday, a beautiful baby sister will come into your world. You won't know it at the time, but she will become your inner family unit; someone who will love you unconditionally, look up to you and make you feel special. She will help you understand what being part of a loving family really means, how important it is to have someone who truly believes in you and has got your back.*

*There will come a time when you are truly content with your life, have reached equanimity and are so grateful for what you have created by yourself, for yourself. You will also be given the most precious gift of all; your own amazing daughter whom you will be able to offer those soothing tones, those loving arms to envelop her in your unconditional love. But before we get to that joyous time, you are going to experience some very dark periods in your life which will cause you distress, make you feel powerless, unseen and unheard. You will hide behind an invisible cloak so the real you becomes more hidden. This will become your greatest survival tool; it will help you to build an inner strength so strong it will stop you from becoming an addict or, even worse, committing suicide.*

*With your infallible inner strength, you will survive being looked upon as different, which will result in you being bullied at secondary school, feeling huge loneliness while at university and eventually removing yourself and your daughter from an emotionally abusive marriage later in life. Know that I am extremely proud of you, as these experiences will define how you become and what you choose to do with your life.*

*The bullying will start around your third year at secondary school – you will feel a misfit, known as Posh Josh, because of how you speak and the way you carry yourself. You will have times when it all gets too much; your self-worth will be extremely low, and you will loathe yourself for being you. However, you'll develop an amazing ability to keep on going, finding the energy to never give up. Also, know the girls who are choosing to behave that way towards you have their own insecurities, and are just trying to make themselves feel better, albeit to your detriment. It says more about them than it does about you. As long as you stay true to yourself, their words and actions won't be able to filter into your inner being.*

*University is the next big leap into adulthood. You will be so excited about the new opportunities going to uni will give you. You choose to study law, a chance to help people, especially children, who are less fortunate than you. This will be important to you because you have a strong desire to want to protect other children from being in situations where they are violated and have no voice. Prepare yourself, my beauty, because receiving your A levels won't be the happy occasion you hope for, and you will not become the lawyer you dreamt of becoming. You will pick yourself up and look back on this, feeling thankful you didn't study law, because you are actually destined for a very different journey; the universe is telling you to help children in a different way, so trust in that and keep listening out for what is your true purpose.*

*Be assured the next turn of events will eventually bring you the love of your life, your daughter. You will feel blessed. She will become your motivation to be the best person you can and, therefore, she will be your greatest teacher.*

*During your last year at uni, you will meet your future husband. He'll whisk you off your feet, treat you like a princess and you* will feel so special, like you finally belong and matter to someone. However, over the coming years, you will learn to your detriment that he is a difficult and controlling man. It will be five years into your marriage, when a Relate counsellor points out that you are in an emotionally abusive relationship, that you will need to draw on your amazing inner strength and launch a project which you will label 'New Life'. It will take you eighteen months to achieve freedom for you and your daughter. Be comforted to know that you will triumph even though there will be days when you feel overwhelmed and spent.

The next eighteen months will require you to dig deep, find your inner strength and grit so you can secure a better life mentally and physically for the two of you. Be assured the deep love you have for your daughter will give you the strength to keep putting one foot in front of the other, so you eventually find a beautiful family home, create financial security and independence by quitting teaching and finding a well-paid corporate job, and build up a new network of friends who will give you the support you need in some of your darkest moments.

Know that what you keep on achieving is phenomenal. You have amazing strength, and I see you as an inspiration in the way you maintain your integrity and are always looking for ways to reframe things, so you can get the best learning out of any situation. Always remember, if you can choose how to respond to a situation, why choose to see it in a negative way when you can see the positive instead?

*Although he will still try to control, manipulate and degrade you, you will rise above it because, by then, you will know you truly deserved to be treated better, and you are worthy of being loved. You will be able to hold your head up high, maintain your dignity, integrity and sheer brilliance – that, he will never be able to take away from you, despite trying. Sadly, that will not be the end of it; you will be forever linked to him because of your daughter. Your next challenge will be to find a way to honour him, show your daughter how to treat people like him with dignity and respect while learning to set and keep new-found boundaries. This won't be easy and you will fall, but don't worry, because I have got you. I promise, eventually, you will come to see him as another of your great teachers, showing you the way to become more resilient, to perfect the way you are able to deal with difficult people and become an even better parent.*

*Embrace your insatiable love of learning and self-development, because this is what will give you the chance to discover your wings, shake off that invisible cloak and find your voice. This enlightened journey will start when a colleague of yours recommends taking a course in Neuro-Linguistic Programming – it will truly change your life and take you out of survival mode. It will help you find the tools you need to flourish and find your authentic self, speak your truth and be the hero in your own story. By finding your true self and holding true to the way you want to parent and live your life, you will enable yourself to find your purpose and start helping other families find a way to flourish too.*

*Please, always remember you are loved and cherished for who you truly are. You are enough!*

*Much love*

X

**What golden nuggets did you learn from this experience?**

Looking back over my life, one of the key things I have learnt is that my parents are doing the best they can; most parents aren't purposefully choosing to harm or damage their children. There comes a point in your adult life when you need to take control, accept your childhood and, as an adult, start making the changes you need to create a fulfilling life. This will involve taking baby steps, and the journey won't be straightforward, but life's not about reaching the final destination, but enjoying the journey, wherever it may take you.

I would also say that valuing yourself and learning to love all of yourself, just the way you are, is key to being content. If I had truly valued myself then I wouldn't have tolerated or thought the abusive behaviour I experienced from my ex-husband was acceptable. You don't have to work for someone's love; love comes naturally and is shown in so many ways which makes you feel special, valued, heard, supported and glowing inside (well that's how I would describe it!). But to experience those things from someone else, you need to feel those things for yourself first. The more love you give, the more you will get back.

Everyone is unique and chooses to deal with life experiences differently. What I have learnt is, the more we can understand and manage our emotions living in the present, the more control and choice we have to make the right decisions. I have found mindfulness to be a great tool for helping me do this.

**What would you tell other women who might be experiencing this?**
*Finding the real you*
By my early twenties, I had moved house so many times that my sister told me she would have to get an address book especially for me. I'd tried numerous jobs ranging from being an air hostess through to a trainee accountant, and still I felt so unhappy. At this point, I realised it wasn't my environment that needed to change, but myself. The mind is extremely powerful and, if you are not careful, your thoughts can consume you. In any situation, you have a choice to either think negatively or positively, so if you have that choice, why not choose positivity every day?

*Being trapped in an emotionally abusive relationship*
Trust your gut instinct, if something doesn't feel right, it generally isn't. As Steve Jobs said: "Don't let the noise of others' opinions drown out your inner voice." This can be very difficult when all your energy is being used up just to navigate the daily obstacle course of avoiding any confrontation. I know you can find that inner strength to change your destiny. Just start taking baby steps, because every goal reached began with those first few steps. Dig deep into your heart and you will find that strength. Believe in yourself!

**What are some of the things you would have changed about the situation if you could?**

Do I wish I had met my husband after I had started all my self-development? Of course, yes! But then I wouldn't have received my greatest gift, my daughter. In life there always has to be a balance – some call it karma – there is always going to be a cause and an effect (an equal and opposite reaction for every action). My life is so much more enriched with my daughter in it that I couldn't be without her.

My early child and adulthood experiences motivated me to make those searches to find a different way of life. And my parents gave me the inner strength to make my own way in the world, eventually being able to do it my way.

**Any final words?**

Life is there for living, the way you want. Being able to reflect on where I have come from and where I am now, I can confidently say, with a smile on my face, I found my way to flourish, and I know you can find yours too. Take your time, trust your instinct and enjoy the journey.

**How can people get in touch?**

- Email: *k_charlton74@hotmail.com*
- LinkedIn: *https://www.linkedin.com/in/kathryn-charlton/*
- Facebook: *https://www.facebook.com/flourishingfamilies/*
- Website: *www.flourishingfamilies.co.uk*

"Don't give up on yourself! You are beautiful and amazing as you are. Embrace life with all it's ups and downs. Every little step is a lesson to your inner happiness. Heal yourself by loving yourself, getting to know yourself."

–Pema Nooten –

# Finding Happiness Through My Inner and Outer Journey

## Pema Nooten

*Visionary, coach, inspirator, motivator, transformational guide, architect of happiness*

What are you passionate about and how are you contributing to the world?

I'm excited to build a global happiness movement to transform the lives of one million entrepreneurs and professionals, leading them from frustration to fulfilment. I founded 'The Architect of Happiness', and I'm passionate about working with entrepreneurs, game-changers and visionaries on increasing happiness at work, personal development and finding joy in life. I love combining my knowledge of Eastern and Western culture, spirituality and art of life, with an active and healthy lifestyle, reading books, meditation and inspirational conversations. I wake up each day with a smile.

There are too many people stuck and frustrated in daily life to feel joy and happiness. This makes me feel sad and passionate at the same time, as I am determined to do something about it with my movement. I believe there are many simple changes you can incorporate in your life by taking small steps. Men and women deserve to live their best lives.

**Describe a pivotal time in your life you wish to share.**
As a young girl, I travelled around the world with my family. I visited many different places in Asia and Europe and encountered many different cultures. I got to see markets full of colourful fruits and vegetables, busy shops with colourful sarees and people negotiating prices. I experienced the hustle and bustle of the city and the smell of good food, the mesmerising beaches, the cold of the mountains and the daily life of the valleys.

I came to love the architecture of old buildings and forgotten histories I followed in the footsteps of the English, Dutch and the Portuguese in South Asia, Malaysia, and Indonesia, the French and Americans in Vietnam.

I learnt there is duality in each country and in every person.

As a baby, I felt the warmth and hospitality of the Indian people. As an adolescent, I watched the smiles of the Thai people. I became curious about what made people live together. How did so many different cultures blend? Are we always changing over time? How can we find happiness within?

Along the way, I practised my languages and cultural traditions, like saying "namaste" in Indian or "sawadee" in Thai. I loved being around the local people and picking up words and phrases I could use. Most of all, I enjoyed the different foods and dishes. The art of cooking and using different spices from around the world is something I still enjoy as an adult woman.

I watched carefully how people lived, how they found peace and mindfulness in their busy lives. I became interested in the smile behind their faces. What made it different for a fisherman from Thailand compared with a Sherpa in Nepal? A fruit seller in the Philippines and an art teacher in Sri Lanka? I learnt there are many different realities, traditions and cultures, each of them as rich as our own. Accepting our own life and making the best out of it was the thread I came to know.

When I got older, I started travelling by myself. There's nothing quite as empowering as travelling in a foreign country by yourself. I love waking up and knowing I have nowhere to be and nobody to see. Taking a bus or walking everywhere. Talking to strangers. Smiling at a nice lady.

Each country I lived in, I embraced with whole my heart. Sometimes I stayed somewhere for a few years, sometimes a few months. This made me flexible. Nothing is as changeable as a human being. Yes, people change like the days. I could easily blend in. At school, in groups and at socials. But blending in has a shadow too. I embarked on a journey to find my own group, my own spot. I asked myself the questions: Where do I stand? What are my desires? I came to know I already had set my first steps.

**Looking back, what made it such an important part of your life journey?**

Slowly I realised my outer journey led me to my inner journey. I never made anywhere my home for long enough. However, I'm grateful for my life, my travels and all my experiences. It all added up to finding my own place and feeling I belonged. It made me search within for the homes of happiness, acceptance and love.

My home of happiness is about loving myself, accepting myself and embracing life at its fullest. It's about the way I feel. By doing so, I am able to connect to people around me, surround myself with inspiration, live a healthy lifestyle by finding inner peace and mindfulness through healthy food, exercises and positivity. How I love sitting in the sun, reading a book, enjoying a coffee and going to a yoga class.

My home of acceptance is about accepting the differences and similarities between you and me. Every person is unique. Every person has talents and qualities that make her or him outstanding. The most beautiful thing is what you can become yourself. It's about valuing your potential. Being yourself works.

My home of love is about loving myself first and enough. I'm okay by myself. I started doing so by finding inner peace and quietness, and by building strong relationships. I started choosing people I wanted to surround myself with in day-to-day life. The love and support of like-minded friends and family can't be undervalued. I'm able to shine my own light now to like-minded people. This is something I share with entrepreneurs, professionals and even the next generation.

For the last decade, I've been focused on my inner journey. I walk a path through personal growth with a learning growth cycle in life lessons. Probably, it's the manifestation of the physical reality of the outer journey. I have an amazing life with travels to beautiful and far-flung places, however, life is not only about the outer journey, I realised. The outer journey sparks and fuels the inner. The outer and inner journey are inextricably connected.

**Based on the wealth of knowledge, wisdom and experience you have now, what would you like to have said to yourself back then?**

*Dear beautiful girl,*

*It will be a sunny, hot afternoon when your baby brother finally comes into the world, filling you with absolute joy and happiness. At only two years old, you are enthusiastic, happy, open and very curious about the world. Entering the hospital room with all your happy feelings to see his little face for the first time, something will happen. An accident. An accident that many children have, and you are no different, but for you, this will be the first taste of unpleasant emotions rising up in your little body, and it won't feel very good. You will drop a jar, a glass jar, and the sound of it will make you feel very frightened, lonely and sad. I want you to know, that I know, you didn't do it on purpose. You weren't in the room to be bad or intentionally hurtful. You were there to meet your newest family member, your little brother.*

*Your dad unfortunately will react like many men. As an adult you'll understand this, but for now know that when a father is taking care of his family and his kids, up all night, worrying about his wife in labour, he can become tired, worried and distracted. So, when that jar breaks, he will not think before he acts, and instead will react with anger. I know this will be the first time you experience this, however I want you to know you are not alone; I'm with you holding your hand right now, comforting you and telling you that you are loved. I know how much you need that right now!*

*I see the tears that come to your eyes, as your eyes widen with fright, and a shadow moves slowly over you. A shadow that you will carry with you, making you feel cold, icy cold, like a wall surrounding you. It is a wall that will need to be brought down. But that's a process that won't happen for many, many years.*

*Although this wall will have its benefits, making you into a strong and independent woman who is always studying, learning and moving on, right now it won't help. The emotions you can't name or fully appreciate, that are too frightening to accept, get stored deep within as your little body feels them boiling inside.*

*Welcoming your baby brother and dropping a glass jar will somehow become connected in your little brain, and you won't fully understand the effects of that until much later. But, for now, just know you will no longer feel the centre of attention, and that won't feel very nice.*

*A few years later, you will welcome your baby sister. This will be a wonderful and joyful event, no dropping jars or being shouted at, no confusion or uncontrolled emotions. You too will be in Asia at that time, in Malaysia. This will be a time you love, playing with your brother and other kids from the neighbourhood, and Indian girls your age. You will even pick up a few Malay words, like "jalan", which means walking.*

*One day you will accidentally throw stones, in great excitement with the other children. It will be a playful act, but it's not appreciated, and yet again you will feel fear. This event will store the idea that playfulness is not accepted firmly in your mind, alongside the idea that accidents can cause you to lose your place as the centre of attention. However, I want you to know, little Pema, that playfulness is totally okay! Kids play and so do you, and all these little connections you are making along your journey are not always quite as they seem.*

*You will eventually leave your beloved Asia, moving back to the Netherlands. This will be a time of going back to school and making friends. You will love school and will make many good friends there and start building your own red suitcase of wonderful, joyful memories. However, not much later, you move with your father, mother, brother and sister back to Thailand, back to a beloved country where you have spent most of your younger years.*

*It was a time without internet, so you spoke with your friends through postcards and letters. Once in a while, you got mail from back home. It was delivered to a post office where you went to collect it once a week. Occasionally, you collected a magazine or schoolbook, posted by good friends. This was your way of feeling connected. I know you also felt connected with a different culture, a different environment. You could easily blend in. You talked easily with different kinds of people. You developed your communication style, along with your curiosity for different places and cultures. How much you loved just walking around and talking to strangers, visiting exciting places and eating colourful fruits. You often went to the market to collect fresh vegetables and other groceries. The smell of fresh sojmilk and home-made Indian food made your mouth water.*

*At fourteen years old you will start turning into a beautiful young woman, something that will be recognised, as you star in a TV commercial. For weeks you were showcased around Bangkok like a movie star. It will be so exciting!*

*One hot June afternoon you will get to travel by yourself, down to the south of the country. This will be a scary moment for you, but you will do it. Your parents will trust you fully and you won't let them down.*

*You will start to do so many things on your own, as you will find it hard to speak up and say what you really feel or want. Without a support group of friends and family around, you will learn to remain silent, feeling you have no choice, but I want to tell you that you do have a choice. The grown-up Pema knows everything about choices. Your independence and silence will eventually make room for warmth and love. Warmth is a deep-rooted value that is totally yours. You love to cuddle and hug your boys and close friends. I say: don't hold yourself back. Spread the* warmth and love around you. There are people who need you, who appreciate your kindness and compassion.

When you and your family move back to the Netherlands for good when you are fifteen years old, it will feel like starting all over. Exciting, making new friends and building that much-needed support network. But, also, trying to figure out your place in a group, as you adjusted from being on your own to be fully supported. From travelling the world, to remaining in one place.

This will all add to your resilience. At the end of your high school year, another baby sister will be born. A blessing for the family, but another opportunity for you to build your wall, covering yourself this time with a blanket of independence, seriousness and being strong. Where did the young, laughing Pema go? Where was she hidden? You had made her smaller and less visible over the years, until much later when you will realise the impact of your blanket.

During your university years, you will slowly start to build a community of your own. Making lasting friends. A time of adventure and discovery, as you discover sharing and being part of a group is very valuable and satisfying. It is something you missed as a young girl. By the time you reach your twenties, you will meet your future husband with whom you will welcome two amazing boys into the world. Your children will ground you, make you tap into your feelings more and help you to remove the blocks of that impenetrable wall you built so long ago, as you start to discover your inner journey. Your children will be a great mirror *for your inner process. They will motivate you to step onto the path of your own emotional transformation.*

*This will have its ups and downs, like divorcing your husband to pursue your own inner happiness. It is a process that will take many years, that will make you frightened and emotional again, lonely, as you ride this process of self-discovery. You will realise that happiness has always been within you. You just have to make a choice by asking yourself the question: "How do you want to live your life? How do you control your own happiness?" You will slowly realise you can put yourself at the centre of your attention, that you never needed anyone else to do it.*

*I will guide you, little Pema, to the safe, beautiful, adventurous places. I will hold your hand every step of the way, so you know you are fine just the way you are; the way you act and the way you move. Everything is fine. There's is no right or wrong. Just acceptance, love and kindness.*

*Too often you showed the world that you were flawless, little girl, maybe in the hope of being liked and accepted. But the reality is you can't please everyone. When you grow up, you will understand and believe the beauty of ourselves is in our vulnerabilities, in our complex emotions and authentic imperfections.*

*Pema, I am able to give this advice to you now as a grown-up, as a woman who has opened her heart to feelings, compassion* and kindness. It is a process of many years, of no longer hiding behind the wall.

As a little girl, you only had your emotions to rely on and what others said, but now I can tell you that when you combine your emotions with thinking and feeling, it will make you an even stronger, more powerful and happy woman. A happy woman, growing yourself, feeling your sexual energy and being proud of your womanhood.

You are a beautiful woman totally in your strength. Yes, life events have triggered you, but coming back to knowing yourself, being yourself, will create trust, self-awareness and self-confidence.

You will fly, creating a busy, full life. Not everybody will understand this. But trust yourself, go for it. How does it feel?

I ask this question Pema, because, without feeling, there is only an empty shell. People need to feel, to open up their hearts and to become the centre of attention. Not selfish, not egoistical, but without self-love it's not possible to really take care of others. I will start to take care of you, Pema, with all my positive intentions; to protect, embrace, hold you.

I will make sure you get all the support you will need to survive and grow. You will grow up, study, fall in love, travel the world, become a mum, and fall in love again. But this time you will fall in *love with yourself. This journey will be like normal relations, with all kinds of ups and downs as you get to know yourself. As your inner journey started, your restlessness to travel and see the world will become a beautiful and valuable journey inwards.*

*As I sit again next to you, my younger self, trying to hold your hand and look into your eyes, I notice this is difficult for you. You have a hard time looking me in the eyes. Is it pain? Loneliness? Anger? Sadness? Or just the unfamiliarity of a loving connection?*

*I know you want to connect, to feel the love. But it feels strange, not common. I whisper in your ear and tell you to take your time, to trust me, to love me and that's okay. It could take days, months or maybe years, and that's totally fine.*

*I see you slowly move your body towards mine, noticing some release, some tension disappearing. I just want to hug you, but your eyes are still looking in all directions. There's little focus. I don't know where you are going with your mind? Where are you, little Pema? What are you feeling?*

*Whatever it is, it's okay. It's okay you don't know. I will continue to caress your hand and give you a kiss on your cheek. I ask you if you are okay with me holding you. And when you say yes, my heart is filled with joy as now you feel safe, and I rock you until you fall asleep.*

*Listen, Pema, while I whisper in your ear: you are good enough, have the courage to rise and fall, to move forward when it gets* rough. *Learn to let your vulnerability show and trust yourself. You don't have to hide any more behind a mask. Your mask has gone, and a beautiful woman has emerged, totally in control and in her power. Be yourself, be kind, find compassion in yourself and share it with others.*

*Sometimes you have to do scary things to grow. Sometimes you have to step outside your comfort zone to realise this. Making a huge jump seems scary at first, but then you realise this is your path. Having the courage to step out and drop your mask makes you a warmer person. I'm there to embrace you, hold you and walk beside you. I'm always there!*

*Embrace life, embrace your life. You're good enough. You're okay and amazing.*

*Happiness lies in the centre of accepting the pain and sadness, and embracing life fully. Happiness is about accepting all parts of yourself and life.*

*Now in your role as an experienced architect of happiness, you are ready to transform frustrations into fulfilment, to unlock your potential, create your happy and healthy life, and help rediscover your core values, coming back to strength and vulnerability in a relaxed way. Live your life out of love. This is your purpose: to create impact through living your best life.*

**What golden nuggets did you learn from your experience?**
- My outer and inner journey are connected and intertwined.
- Show emotions, show vulnerability.
- My experience with different cultures and countries has made me more open. I also understand that it's sometimes difficult to really open up for things differently.
- Love yourself first to love others.
- There's no right or wrong, just love and kindness.
- True happiness is about embracing myself fully. My emotions, my warmth, my seriousness. All my shades.
- I'm the driver of my own bus of happiness. Only I know what I feel, what I value.
- Being successful is doing what makes me happy.
- Trusting my inner fire and strength is sometimes scary. Don't self-reject. Embrace your power. This makes me feel more energised and happy.
- Seize this moment to start your inner journey. Don't wait for the perfect place and time.
- Talk to people about my fears and feelings
- Dedicate regular time to relaxation, mindfulness and a healthy lifestyle.

**What would you tell other women who might be experiencing this?**
Don't give up on yourself! You are beautiful and amazing as you are. Embrace life with all its ups and downs. Every little step is a lesson to your inner happiness. Heal yourself by loving yourself, getting to know yourself, by getting to know yourself step by step, and a little more every day you will become your own champion and happiness architect. Life isn't easy for anyone. You and I are capable of feeling

joy, happiness, pain and grief. Learn how to deal with everyday challenges, frustrations and your potential. Be grateful for what you have, count your blessings, love your friends and family. Be grateful for all the lessons in life. When you are frustrated about life, go back to your happy memories and rediscover your core values. What did you like doing as a kid? What made you happy?

If you are experiencing fear, loneliness, frustration, lack of self-confidence, unhappiness, nervousness or lack of love and attention, I would suggest taking the path of self-discovery and self-healing. Be an architect of your own life. Only you can take charge of your life. Only you are totally responsible for your own happiness and success. Don't wait for others to make you happy. Start by loving yourself and embark on your own inner journey. It only takes one little step to take you in the right direction. At one point you'll look back and see you've taken many steps, and that gives so much joy and inner strength. That inner strength will set you on fire. The fire of life will set things in motion even more. Don't be afraid of your inner fire. Your inner fire is the engine of your happiness.

**What are some of the things you would have changed about your situation if you could?**
There are not many things I would have changed in my situation. I believe that all my golden nuggets, life events and pivotal moments add up to who I am today. I could have asked for support at certain moments. I could have been more open and vulnerable at an earlier stage to people around me. I could have been more mindful and started meditating as a younger woman.

**Any final words?**

I love my family, my outer and inner journey, my boys, and my love. Without you I am not the person I am today. I'm glad that you are in my life. Thank you for being my grounded base and my mirror. I'm grateful for my life and all the lessons I learnt.

I wish that you will live your life to the fullest. I wish you a beautiful and happy life, a life you embrace fully. An ocean of happiness lies within you. You only have to see and feel what's there. Choose it today. Be brave. What are you waiting for?

**How can people get in touch with you and see the work you do?**

People can get in touch with me via

- LinkedIn: *linkedin.com/in/pemanooten*
- Website: *www.thearchitectofhappiness.com*
- Instagram: *@thearchitectofhappiness*
- Facebook: *Pema Nooten, thearchitectofhappiness*

"Your path is very much influenced by who you let surround you. Let God guide it. Sit in silence and let His prescence be enough. When you remove bad things, energy and people and you say no to accepting certain behaviours the right, good and beautiful people will be able to enter your space, life and heart."

– Rochelle Nicole –

# When You Stop Running ...

**Rochelle Nicole (Smethurst)**

*Mirror mentor and master trainer of online freedom*

W hat are you passionate about and how are you contributing to the world?

My heart sings when I help the lonely feel loved, find their way and know there is hope. Too many people are living with their heads down, lonely, depressed, hating their life, their careers, their home, their future, and hating on themselves. They are not living consciously and not even giving themselves time and space to look themselves in the mirror, right in the eye, and give LOVE and RESPECT for all they have survived. I am on a mission to help more women to look in the mirror and love what they see. Mentally, emotionally, physically, spiritually. Free yourself.

**Describe a pivotal moment in your life you wish to share:**
When I first started writing this chapter, I thought of one pivotal moment in my life at twelve years old I wished to share but, as I continued to write, I saw several pivotal moments that have changed and shaped my life.

I still remember the night before my first pivotal moment. Lying on a mattress on my auntie's spare room floor, I couldn't sleep. All I could hear was the sound of my dad in the single bed next to me, sobbing. I remember it so vividly. I was twelve years old. He was heartbroken. My mum and he were over. It broke my heart.

I didn't originally know what prompted his reaction the next day, but recently found out, as we left my auntie's house the next morning, two of my aunts told him to "suck it up" and "get over it." He replied: "What's the point? May as well end it for us all." Dad told her she would never see us again and drove off with my brother and I in the car. My auntie rang my mum. My mum rang the police. They were now on a murder-suicide hunt.

I remember stopping at payphones along the Central Coast that day, as there were no mobile phones back then. He would call my mum, getting really angry if he heard "beeping" through the phone, as that meant the police were tapping it to trace our location. She would promise they weren't, but Dad would hear the beep, lose his temper, hang up and we would speed off again.

The last time we stopped at a payphone before they successfully traced us, he was talking to the police this time and he was ANGRY. I remember him getting back in the car and speeding off SO fast. My brother was in the front seat, our puppy and I in the back. Dad sped around the corner and down the hill. My brother pointed at a police car coming towards us, saying: "Dad they spotted us!" As Dad looked in the rear-view mirror, I turned around to see they had done a U-turn and were chasing after us. Dad took a quick left turn up the first street he saw, but at the top of the hill was a dead end, leading into the bush.

We were in the local area we grew up in, so it was no coincidence (although very crazy timing) that someone Dad hadn't seen for twenty years pulled up to visit someone in the street and asked Dad what he was doing. When he explained that we were "hiding from the cops," the guy offered us a lift out.

I still remember leaving our puppy in the car and, as we drove out of the street, the police car drove up. For them to find our abandoned car, dog and belongings with no sign of my dad, myself or my brother, you can imagine they could only assume we had run into the bush. It was like a Sliding Doors moment.

While writing this, I have called both my mum and dad to ask their version of this day, and when I asked Dad "what would you have done if your friend hadn't come up the street?" he replied he would have waited until the cops pulled up beside him to question him, and then he was going to take off.

Dad: "I know all the back roads. I would have gone till I stacked it."

Me: "You would have gone on a police chase until we crashed?"

Dad: "Yeah, pretty lucky we didn't, hey?" he laughed.

My dad is reckless, fearless and ruthless. He was only thinking of revenge that day. I have no doubt God sent that man up that street that day, saving us from a police chase ending in tragedy. This was the first pivotal moment in my life.

The second pivotal moment was when I was twenty-six years old and I found the strength to leave my long-term partner, my fiancé. It wasn't a relationship that allowed me to be myself or grow personally or professionally. It had grown into a relationship filled with jealousy, abuse and drugs, and it was not the future I was working so hard for.

The third pivotal moment was when I was twenty-eight years old and a friend took his life. Suicide is not something you ever can prepare yourself for. Rhys was someone I had been friends with for three years but, in that time, we had a bond no one else knew.

The fourth and most important pivotal moment happened in July 2017 when I was in America and gave my life to Christ. I was lonely, depressed and suicidal myself. I had given up hope of a future; I couldn't see anyone ever loving me. I had terminated my pregnancy only months earlier, and had never felt so alone, broken and unloved in my life.

I was taken to a coffee shop for 'Bible study', which I was not very excited to attend, but what I found was a Starbucks table with seventeen women sitting around having coffee and talking so casually about life.

I started to hear their hard life stories and what they had been through, yet they said they knew God had been watching down on them, guiding them, and the support they gave one another with so much faith and glory to God inspired me like never before.

They asked me my story and I burst into tears, explaining everything to them. When they explained God was the Holy Spirit, full of love, hope, peace, and He is a Father with a BEAUTIFUL future planned for me, I believed them.

At this point in my life I had NOTHING else, only the two red suitcases I was running away around the world with, so why would I not say yes and BELIEVE in this? If this is the miracle they speak of, I am all in!

It saved my life.

**Looking back, what made it such a pivotal part of your journey?**
When Dad went on the run with us that day, it taught me to run. Anytime something in my life gets too hard or I don't like it, I run. I don't usually tackle it head-on. I will cause chaos and then run!

I would work a job for eighteen months (excel, smash it, make waves, hit targets, succeed), then I would run. Be in a relationship, gets too hard, not going how I think it should go, don't believe he will love me, sabotage it, and run. The same for friendships, too. I was SO much in survival mode that I never stopped for a second to breathe, think or get help. I would just run. I was like a tornado!

Walking away from a long-term relationship, a house you owned and a potential marriage was a HUGE turning point. I had so many people say how brave I was. Not many people would do that, but I was so unhappy in that relationship. Always being questioned, emotionally blackmailed, blamed, given ultimatums. This absolutely shaped my future as an adult and gave me strength to walk away from someone or something that didn't serve me. You are better off being single than being married to someone who doesn't allow you to be YOU.

Rhys's suicide was like a ripple effect. I don't remember ever having thoughts of suicide, even in my darkest days as a child, but all of a sudden when things got tough and one friend had done it, others were saying it, and you start to think: "I get it. Rhys. I know why you did it; it would be easier than life right now." I wish I knew the love of God back then, so I could tell Rhys. I wish I had the lifestyle I live now, without drugs, parties and alcohol. I wish I could have shown Rhys this way.

Deciding to become a follower of Jesus is a spiritual journey I didn't even know I was on for so many years. Starting to see "the universe" guiding me and knowing I was meeting people and having experiences that were all leading to the next moment were happening every day. But, like a slap in the face, I learnt and felt that God created the universe and can give me new light and hope for a future, which is one thing I never saw for myself. This pivotal moment is the one that changed the course of my life forever.

**Based on the wealth of knowledge, wisdom and experience you have now, what would you like to say to yourself back then?**

*Baby girl, when you stop running, you will know who you are.*

*When you stop running, you will know what you want. When you stop running, you will have the confidence to wear what you want, do what you want, be who you want. When you stop running, you won't have to impress anyone but yourself.*

*You WILL impress yourself. You will love yourself. You will know yourself. You will be so proud of yourself. You will inspire yourself.*

*But you don't know this yet, because you are only a child.*

*You are about to experience things most people will never even fathom experiencing as a child. You will continue to run throughout your life; you are like a whirlwind. Every eighteen months you will get a new job. You're good at them: smash goals, make friends, hit targets, then quit. You move on.*

*You will travel. A lot. That's not a bad thing. But, boy, are you running. Country after country. City after city. New friendships, new relationships. You don't even remember half the people you meet.*

*You're like a tornado. Hardly conscious. Living unconsciously. Running through life.*

*You call yourself the freedom chaser for many years; you just want to be free from pain. You don't have to chase it, you don't have to run; He is with you and He is the ultimate definition of freedom. You won't know, until you stop running. I want to tell you not to worry, I am with you every step of the way. But for now, baby girl, it's time to run! Are you ready?*

*Shit is about to hit the fan! You're starting to become aware of things. Things don't seem right. You're twelve years old and, when you wake up for school, your dad is drinking Jim Beam cans for breakfast. You know he works hard? You know he works the night shift? Your mum will explain his behaviour by telling you the morning after his night shift is like the evening for most people, so that's why he drinks bourbon for breakfast. So, this is normal, right? Well, it's our normal.*

*You find out later in life, he hadn't been at work. He didn't work nights, he just hadn't slept yet. Mum hid it from you so well. Dad was spending a lot of time in the back shed. You have no idea why until your mum leaves. Your mum will be the holder of the "normality strings" and, when she goes, your dad will have free range to do what he wants, and this is where you will learn about another side of life. Dad will open up the house to drug addicts and dealing. It always had been like this, but not so obvious. It was always 'out the back'. You're about to REALLY see it for all it is.*

*Your dad will get a girlfriend. She will be a hooker. She will become your stepmum. She will put you on the pill, "'cos she was having sex at your age." You'd think she would have taught you what not to do, but this is all she knows. But don't worry, baby girl, you are safe. I am with you the entire way. God is looking over us and we are protected (it's the ONLY explanation for how you survive this life!).*

*Baby girl, DoCS[1] are going to come to you at school. They will ask if you're safe and want to stay with your dad. You will say yes. But you don't have to do that! Tell them you're scared and you're not safe (you don't see it now, but you will see it when you stop running). This is such an unsafe environment for you. Drug use, in front of you. A lot of it. A lot of men and women coming and going. You will witness overdoses, pretty girls, lots of them. You will get angry with your dad.*

*But he will brush off your emotions as if they don't matter as he tells you it's all fine and, "that wasn't meant to happen." One night you even watch him drag the overdosed body of his friend through the hallway of a hotel room you're staying in, and down into the street, while the hotel staff are yelling at us all to leave. The ambulance will come, but the guy won't make it. He will die that night. You watch it unfold on the street below from the hotel room window above.*

*And the following day you will go to school, like any other normal day. You will then go home to your auntie's house. That's where you live; your stepmum dropped you off once, said she would be back in two weeks but, baby girl, she doesn't come back. It isn't*

---

1  Department of Community Services (Australia)

*because you weren't loved; your dad went to jail and you're better off without the hooker. Trust this process.*

*You will have to act like a normal schoolkid. But this is not normal, beautiful girl. It's okay to know it's not. You are SO strong. You are SO brave. You won't tell anyone what is happening because you want to protect your dad. You don't want anyone to hate him any more than they already do.*

*But listen, you don't have to protect him, baby girl; if only you would do something about it, you would be protected too. You hid it all so well. You want so badly to have a mum to go clothes shopping with, to give you advice on what to wear, borrow her clothes or help her choose hers. Whenever you see mothers and daughters shopping together, your heart breaks into a thousand pieces. But you have a voice; tell these ladies how lucky they are, because you don't want them to take it for granted.*

*The windows in your house are never open. The blinds always closed. This house will be the worst you live in based on what you experience. But it is you and Dad against the world. Your brother is sixteen, so it is easy for him to jump on his bike and see Mum without Dad knowing.*

*Dad is your only form of stability. You feel safe with him. You can't see how bad it is or how scary for everyone else to have to sit back and watch. You are HIS baby girl. You will blame yourself for so long when your mum leaves. You felt that because your dad hadn't let you go back to your mum after school holidays and made you tell her you didn't want to go home, she wouldn't have gone off the rails. But, baby girl, you find out when you stop running, she was taking drugs well before you left. This was not your fault. She didn't start when you left or after that day of the police chase. For ALL of your teens and twenties, you blame yourself. You thought that when she lost you is when she lost herself because, at forty-one years old, she met someone that allowed her the drug addiction your dad tried to keep her from. For all those years you blamed him, the man who would become your stepdad. But it was only his influences; your mum wanted to do it. Watching Dad all those years made her want drugs too. Crazy to believe; you either learn from mistakes or are led into them. Your mum didn't learn; she was the lead.*

*She was the most innocent woman, who didn't swear, hardly drank and didn't smoke. She wasn't a drug addict. But soon she will be living on the streets, begging for money, cigarettes and her next hit! Talk about heartbreaking and life-changing. When you reach your eighteenth birthday your aunties will comment: "We are so proud of you. We didn't think you'd make it." Although quite a back-handed compliment, I want you to know, YOU were always going to make it! You're a strong, incredible woman.*

*Don't worry, baby girl; I am there, holding your hand, loving on you, keeping you safe. You will crave stability your entire life, but you don't get it. You CAN have it, but instead you will choose to keep running.*

*You will have a fiancé. You are in love for so long but, over time, you realise he does not lift you up, but tries to bring you down. He tells you what you can and can't wear, who you can talk to, goes through your phone, accuses you of cheating, asks where you were when you're at the hair salon too long. These traits are not okay, baby girl. Although you buy a house together, are engaged and your whole life is his friends, you will find the strength to leave.*

*You know he does not make your heart happy and, now you are both taking drugs at parties every weekend, you know this has to end. The only time you get along is when you're on drugs now. This is not how it is meant to be. You have to walk away and you do. You know it is so hard to leave, but it is so much harder to stay.*

*Leaving your fiancé didn't mean you were leaving the drugs behind. In fact, it fuelled it. You will find a love for the party scene and do it solidly for two years. Although for a very long time you will say things like, "I don't want to do drugs, my parents did that," you will soon realise you can escape your reality through drugs, and it's an addiction you find yourself loving in the first year, but knowing you need to stop by the second.*

*Baby girl, you don't have to take drugs to escape! I wish you had better influences around you, stopping you, helping you. Some tried, but you didn't listen. You were all in. You start to tell yourself you are addicted, but it will not keep you. You will not be like your parents. You have a rule: as long as it doesn't impact your Monday to Friday job, it's fine. And then comes Monday, and staring at yourself shaking, looking in the mirror, telling yourself "you have to stop."*

*You're tiny; the drugs are eating away at you. You know it will never take hold, though; you know you will never be like them. You hit an all-time low when you meet a fresh-out-of-jail guy and fall 'madly in love'. Boy, that is a rollercoaster. It was filled with anger, fear, torment and BAD drugs. He would leave, get in fights and come back to your house. You'd lock the doors, but find him sleeping on your front door every morning. The 'love' you have for this man is a HEART OF HELP. You want to help him so bad, but you are so scared at the same time. This man is not good for you. Enough is enough. You can't do this any more. It's okay, God knew; He already had it planned.*

*After being threatened, this guy will keep your passport so you can't go. You escape this vicious cycle, get your passport and move to London. Talk about running, huh?! You can't get much further than the other side of the world, baby girl. The thing about running is, wherever you go, you go with YOU. You can run, but until you deal with what's happened in your world, life and past, you cannot fix this pain.*

*You PROMISE yourself no drugs when you go. If you take drugs you will have a relapse, come down hard and move back home, and that would be failing. You told the world you're moving to London for two years, and that's what you will do. You sold everything you own (all except your bed, the one thing you never had of your own as a child, so you ensure you do as an adult).*

*Moving to London solo was by far the best thing you could do for yourself. It is where you find your love for physical health and personal development, where you find your inner strength.*

*It was tough, but you do it, baby girl, and all on your own. Find a job, a home, money, friends. You started fresh and you made it a success. You inspire so many people with this journey. You move back to Australia at twenty-nine years old, ready to take on your home country and show them how far you've come. You dream that you are going to meet your soulmate, settle down and have a family.*

*But here is the problem; you're working in a job you hate. You're trying to be healthy. You're training daily. But it all comes crashing down. You don't love yourself. You don't look in the mirror and love what you see. So how can someone else love you? They try, but you don't believe it. You sabotage any man or relationship that comes near you. You haven't healed. You love, and you love hard, but YOU DON'T KNOW HOW TO BE LOVED!*

*You don't know where to live. You try Bondi, then the other side of Sydney. This job, and that job. This guy and that guy. Nothing works. You're still running. Remember how strong you were in London? What happened? You turn thirty, and you're so lost. Again!*

*You haven't seen Rhys since you got back from London, but you're both planning it. It's Tuesday morning and you're chatting to him. He tells you he's struggling with uni, and has to resit an entire unit he failed. "You'll be okay!" It's not what he needs to hear, baby girl; ASK if he is okay. Is there anything you can do to help? Understand his pain and his feelings! On the Friday night, he will take his life.*

*Baby girl, it's normal to feel blame, hurt and confusion. Why didn't you see the signs? Something happens from this event in your life; you want to share your heart and tell people this isn't the way. Suicide is not the answer. You become a voice for this movement and you go on to raise more than $120,000 for the Movember Foundation.*

*This is what happens, baby girl; you are so fucking good at everything you do, and you don't even know it. How can you not see these amazing traits within yourself? You want to spread the word of faith and love (although you don't know it yet, that's what is guiding you), and you do it with ease!*

*But, baby girl, wait! You're about to run. You leave a job, a boyfriend. You are broken, your heart never healing, your brain never stopping, your world never stops spinning and you run again. This is the time where it all becomes too much. You are now the face of the Movember Foundation. You have people reaching out, suicidal. You don't know how to deal with it, because you haven't taken time to heal YOU. And now you will want to take your own life. You're thirty-one years old and don't see why you should live. You know why Rhys did it. Life is too hard! You won't believe you would ever be a good mum, have a future or find a man who will love you. What is the point of living? You get it. You don't feel like you can be yourself, because they definitely won't love you if you are being you!*

*All these are lies you will tell yourself over and over again. The whirlwind of your life will keep swirling and swirling and you* will want it to stop, reaching a point where you decide to stop it yourself. You will research it. How many of your antidepressants would you need to take, to not feel any more, to not wake up? But then you will decide another country will help, and your whirlwind will kick off again. Packing your bags and booking your flight to Bali, you're on the road to building your online business, and that you do!

Baby girl, I want to let you know, you're very good in business, very hard-working, target-focused. You can and do build that business. But, God knows, you're running and you're running hard now. He knows because He is chasing you, and He has other plans.

This is your last run, baby girl, 'cos He catches you! God chases you down, and in the most random place. You are in Riverside, California, with a bunch of women you don't even know. You lay it all down, finally give up on running, and know you can't do it on your own any more. You want the one and only Father in your life to guide you, hold you, love you, and take everything you have to be His.

The pain, suffering, loneliness, doubt, insecurities, they are His to take. It's like the weight of the world has been lifted this day, baby girl, and boy does it feel good. You cry and cry and cry! And you leave that coffee shop with a sense of belonging, lightness and hope. It's not up to you when you die. You don't choose when you go to heaven. God has a plan for you, and He will decide when your time is up!

*Through Him you discover forgiveness. You forgive your mum and dad. You don't blame them any more. You will love on them and pray for their salvation, for they have a story too.*

*You will discover through Him, how to love, how to have faith, how to have hope. One day you will meet a guy who is amazing, kind, gentle, loving, trusting. That's what you need and it's okay to fall in love, to wear your heart on your sleeve. Don't let anyone tell you otherwise. You have a heart. Let it feel. He will love your skin, freckles and curly hair because he sees what God sees. You're beautiful and pure.*

*You're perfect as you are. You are enough. It is okay to let someone provide it for you, with you, beside you. It is okay for someone to love you, take care of you. Let them in. It is possible they love you.*

*Respect your money. You're allowed to save. Don't believe the lie of "you can't take it when you die." You can't take it when you die, no, but you can leave a legacy. A legacy to your children. Yes, you are going to have children, and you're going to be an amazing mum! I don't know when – our story isn't finished yet – but you're going to have a family. You'll be an amazing mum! You're going to grow old with your husband. You do find one and he loves you for exactly who you are, every inch of who you have become!*

*There is a brighter life, baby girl. Don't give up hope; you'll survive this.*

*Baby girl, unlike when you were growing up, there is brightness, sunlight. There is a brighter life waiting for you when you stop running.*

*Lots of love, your thirty-three-year-old, beautiful, solid, centred, grounded, conscious, content, faith-filled, confident, loving self.*

**What golden nuggets did you learn from your experience?**
I learnt it is okay and possible to be loved. You don't have to keep moving. Make your house your home. Slow down, make conscious decisions. Listen to your heart. I learnt to save money and not burn it. Set yourself up, build for your future. Leave a legacy.

**What would you tell other women who might be experiencing this?**
Talk to God; you're not alone. Running is exhausting, and while I don't take back any of my running 'cos I saw the world and met amazing people, I also pushed a lot away along the journey. Be careful who you let in, but also be mindful of who you push away. Remove all, clear your mind, heal and then be diligent in who you let back in. Your path is very much influenced by who you let surround you. Let God guide it. Sit in silence and let His presence be enough.

When you remove bad things, energy and people and say no to accepting certain behaviours, the right, good and beautiful people will be able to enter your space, life and heart.

**What are some of the things you would have changed about your situation if you could?**

I know a lot of people say "I would never change a thing," but there are absolutely some things I would change. I would have given time to Rhys, simply ask if he was okay, to lead him to a healthier life and to Christ.

I would not have given my dignity out so freely. If only I felt self-love and was shown, inspired or guided by better influences in my life, I wouldn't have gone to find it in that way.

I wouldn't have been so brutal and savage in my running, for that hurt people along the way.

With saying all of that, I do know these experiences are absolutely who we are moulded to be, and it has all led me to this place of total mental, physical, emotion and spiritual peace and strength. And for that I am grateful.

**Any final words?**

I truly, with all my heart, thank God for looking out for me, for always being there for me. What other explanation do I have? How does a girl, all of twelve, twenty and thirty years, survive the above? I pray every day over little kids I see in the same environment I grew up in. I know God has them; I just pray they see, feel and accept Him sooner than I did, then they won't have to run so tirelessly for so long.

Now, I've stopped running. Life is calm, beautiful, full of belief and I have the clearest vision for a bright and family-filled future.

**How can people get in touch with you and see the work you do?**
- Website: *www.rochellenicole.com.au*
- Instagram: *@rochellenicolee*
- Facebook: *Rochelle Nicole*

"As conscious adults, it is our duty to break the cycle of negativity that does not serve us. We are not responsible for the programming we picked up as children, but we are 100% responsible for fixing it as adults. I have learned that when you learn to love yourself, your whole world changes."

– Grace Van Berkum –

# "Anything and Everything is Possible"

### Grace Van Berkum

*Holistic nutritionist, raw food chef, nutrition coach, yoga and meditation teacher*

**W**hat are you passionate about and how are you contributing to the world?

I am passionate about helping people become better versions of themselves, changing their health and their futures. I teach people how the foods they eat affect the vibrations they put out into the world, and how life matches those vibrations back into their lives. Our outer reality reflects our inner reality. I am passionate about teaching people the foods we eat affect how we handle stress, deal with our emotions, and perceive our lives. I help people connect the dots with what they eat and how that affects their health, and how their food and lifestyle choices affects the health of the planet. I love helping people transform their existence, the way they carry themselves physically and mentally, by living more consciously, mindfully, and with awareness. I love teaching people how eating high-vibrational, fresh foods from mother earth are a way to love ourselves and our bodies, and to connect to healing nature. I love teaching people how our bodies want to thrive, want to be in balance, and want to heal! We just have to treat our bodies with love and respect and it quickly will regain its strength and vitality.

**Describe a pivotal moment in your life you wish to share.**

My very first memory of my life was of screaming. It wasn't my own, it was a woman's. A woman with a thick European accent who was extremely angry. And it was more than just screaming at the top of her lungs, it was more like a shrill. And it wouldn't stop. I was in the bathtub with my brother and I just wanted to play. Even at a young age, I was annoyed that this woman screaming was ruining my bathtub play time with my brother. So, I just kept turning on the water to drown out the shrills. And we continued to play. That was our game. Hear a scream, turn on the tap. Hear a scream, turn on the tap. My little brother, who was two years old, thought it was funny. We both thought it was even funnier when the water started to overflow all over the floor. So, we kept doing it of course! Eventually the screaming woman brought her wretched, annoying screams inside the bathroom where she shockingly discovered there was water everywhere. (This did not help the screaming situation!)

And this first memory of life was just foreshadowing what lay ahead of me. Little did I know at three years old this would be the norm in my life – wretched, daily screaming and me, little Gracey, making a game out of it to keep myself happy, and also to protect my brother. For this woman, the screamer, was my own mother. And I was about to go on a roller coaster of a childhood that would impact me for a lifetime.

**Looking back, what made it such a pivotal part of your journey?**
Without having gone through what I did as a child, and also as an adult, I wouldn't be able to understand what rock-bottom really means, and what it takes to become healthy and strong. I wouldn't have had the opportunity to relearn how to live and eat in a way that is healthy and balanced. Relearning how to eat as an adult, plus learning how to live with more love for myself and others, has given me a gift of empathy and compassion for my clients. Many clients come to me who are sick; their health is suffering, or they are lost in their lives, and need help completely changing their lifestyle and nutrition to change their direction or their future. Having gone through what I have gone through, I completely understand what it takes. My personal experiences of changing my health, combined with my holistic nutrition knowledge makes me an excellent and supportive nutrition coach and holistic nutritionist for those ready to transform and try a different approach to living and eating. I understand my clients, because I have been in their shoes.

**Based on the wealth of knowledge, wisdom and experience you have now, what would you like to say to yourself back then?**

*Darling three-year-old Gracey,*

*I want you to know something, as you are about to go through years and years of pain.*

*You are so tough. Even as a child you are so tough and strong. Somewhere inside you, you already know you have to endure these extremely unpleasant times and, one day, you won't have to any more. Somewhere inside of you, you know this inflicted pain one day will pass. Somewhere inside of you, you know that this woman, your mother, is not well. You know the things she screams at you for do not make sense. No one has told you this, but somewhere inside of you, you know something is not right. As you grow older, you will go through a lot of confusing times, pain and suffering. Everyone wants to love their own mother, and you are no different. Even when she hurts you so much, you will still yearn to love her. This will cause great pain and confusion for you, because the woman you love so much also hurts you so much. Darling Grace, unfortunately your own mother will hurt you every day. Not just physically, but also emotionally. Get ready.*

*She will say the meanest things to you. That you should die. That she will kill you by shooting your head off in the middle of the night. That she will burn your bed. That you are hideous. That no one will ever love you. That you don't deserve to live. That your life means nothing. That you will never amount to anything. That she brought you into this world and that she can take you out.*

*These are things you will hear every day. Her words will hurt you so much more than being hit across the face and body time and time again. Her words will hurt more than all the times she repeatedly spits on your face. You will have to be a brave little girl, sweet Gracey, to get through this pain. And the only way you will know how to survive all of this is to disconnect from your reality. You will learn to disconnect from your feelings and sensations of being struck, so your little heart does not hurt. These are the survival skills you will learn already, at three years old.*

*Darling six-year-old Gracey: You will be taken to foster homes and police stations numerous times in your childhood. You will always do your best to not cry. At six years old, you will be tough and strong so no one else can hurt you. You will do everything in your power to protect your brother. You will even try your hardest to take care of your mother when her anger turns into deep depression and episodes of sobbing for days and nights. You will try to soothe her and caress her and make her eat food when she is so sad like this. You will have no time to play with dolls and other kids. You are already an adult at such a young age. You will have a very important job to do, even at that age, and that is to take care of your family. To endure extra physical and mental abuse to protect your brother. To be the bodyguard and spokesperson for you and your brother, in front of your mother, the police officers, social workers, teachers, foster parents and, one day, in front of the lawyers in a court of law.*

*Sweet Gracey, your strength became evident from the moment your life began. And this strength will take you far into your life. This strength will later be a foundation, a conduit, a bridge, for your own healing. And through the journey of your own healing, you will be able to guide others to their own healing. But you need to be a strong little girl to get through this first.*

*There will be times you will be locked in closets and rooms for days. Your potty will become so overflowing with pee and poo, you will start to defecate on the floor because there will be nowhere else to go. And, of course, being the bright light you are, you will take this awful, stinky situation and make a game out of it! You will keep you and your brother occupied to pass the time being locked up, by creating poo murals all over the walls and TV! What a creative, funny, and positive little six-year-old you are! There will be another time when you are locked up and, fed up at being in your 'prison', you will open the window from the second floor and jump out. Yes, you will have no fear, and jump out the window to the unknown! You will jump to escape the madness! You will jump to find help! But, unfortunately, the help won't come yet. So, hang in there little Gracey. You still have many more years of this life ahead.*

*Darling nine-year-old Gracey: You are so tough, but you will be sad. This woman, your mother, will deny you a childhood, and as you get older, you will start to get angry.*

*Extremely angry!*

*But you will not be able to express it, for this life you have to endure is a big, shameful secret. No one can know what is happening to you. NO ONE. And this secret, and this anger, will burn inside you as a teenager and young adult, scarring you, choking you, because you will not be able to understand or decipher it. You will desensitize yourself so much as a child, because you will be beaten for expressing yourself, so you will not be able to understand this anger as you start to mature. So, the only way you will know to deal with this burning anger, pain and confusion that will take over your entire body, is to numb it.*

*Brace yourself, darling sixteen-year-old Gracey. You will go through much of your childhood, teenage and young adult years with addictions. All sorts of addictions – addicted to copious amounts of sugar, to food, binge eating, throwing up, starving yourself, exercise, to the scale as a measure of self-worth, to alcohol, drugs, to anything that will numb you from your own, extreme self-hatred and self-loathing. Your addictions will be the only way you will know how to survive, to control at least some part of your life, because you can't control the pain being inflicted on you by your crazy mother.*

*You will be so sad at times that you will want to kill yourself. You will imagine all the ways you would do it and the sadness it would bring to others when they find out you are dead. Imagining your death will bring you such joy. While other girls daydream about what to wear to the high school dance or which boy they have a crush on, you will daydream about how people would discover your dead body. Luckily for you, you will never actually go through with it.*

*Oh, twenty-nine-year-old Gracey: hang in there, you will get through all this, I promise! You will move from pain to pain to pain, hit many rock-bottoms, each one worse than the other, you will get extremely sick and heartbroken from how you are living your life, suffer from deep depression and anxiety, you will hate yourself every second of the day, desperately want to kill yourself but never have the guts to go through with it, cry yourself to sleep nearly every night but brave a stoic face by day, you will keep doing drugs and keep doing drugs and keep doing drugs, you won't be able to recognize yourself in the mirror. And then, one scary, blessed day, everything will change.*

*Your rock-bottom will be so bad that the only way to get through will be to surrender to the unknown, to the possibilities of a new way of living, to a force greater than yourself. You will have to try a new approach to life because, clearly, nothing else you have tried is working for you.*

*And through this surrender, this smashing of your heart into a million little pieces to create an opening, you will begin to find freedom. Freedom from the lies you have been brainwashed with, from the self-hatred that you have been taught by your mother, who also hated herself.*

*The shattering of your life will eventually lead you to a place of peace. You will take all the broken pieces of yourself and slowly put them together piece by piece, and this is how you will find inner peace. You will embark on a journey of making peace with your pieces. This surrender into the unknown will begin to uncover the real you, the true you, the you filled with hope, trust, joy and love. Through this surrender, and courageously walking this path of inner truth and self-realisation, you will begin to change the direction of generations of trauma and pain within your family.*

*Hang in there, thirty-year-old Gracey. Buckle your seat belt. This will not be easy, but you must get through it. Have courage and go* deep, without the numbing and crutches. It is through this time of sobriety, not just from alcohol and drugs, but sobriety from the bullshit you have been fed by your mother and bullshit you have believed about yourself, that you will find the meaning of your life. You must get through this. The memories of pain and trauma and abuse from such a young age will all start to bubble up to the surface. It will petrify you. You will be scared to get close to people because you believe everyone will ultimately hurt you. And you never want to experience such pain from another human being again.

Keep uncovering all the layers of yourself. Keep doing the inner work. You are on the right path, Gracey. This is the only way to heal your heart so you can help the world.

Learning how to feel will be the hardest thing you have ever done. Learning how to communicate will be the hardest thing you have ever done. Trying to figure out who you really are will be the hardest thing you have ever done. Learning how to eat will be the hardest thing you have ever done. Learning how to live with love, for yourself, and also for others, will be the hardest thing you have ever done.

But you need to do it. There is no other way.

I believe in you, thirty-five-year-old Gracey. In these crucial years, you will start to understand that without self-love, you will never release the pain. You will slowly begin to understand the only way to release the shackles of your mother's voice is to give yourself *the love and compassion she was never capable of giving you. Or give to herself.*

*You will start to learn boundaries. You will start to learn when to say no. And also when to say yes. You will start to move through your own fear that used to paralyse you. The power you never had as a child will start to grow as an adult. You will start to love yourself. And it will be hard! But the more you find love within you, the more your life changes for the better. The more you find love within you, your perception of life changes. You will discover that learning to love yourself will change your reality! Self-love will become your path, always a work in progress, but this commitment to your personal growth will help you become free from your own inner turmoil. This path of self-love will light the way for not only yourself, but also others.*

*It's not over yet, darling forty-one-year-old Gracey. But hang in there; you are getting there.*

*One day, the one thing you wished for your entire life, that your mother would die, will finally happen. It won't be pretty. You will find her dead body in her apartment. It will be shocking yet relieving, sad yet comforting, all wrapped into one bundle of emotions, and this intertwinement of opposites will bring you such immense guilt.*

*On the day they are supposed to cremate her, you will suddenly stop everything and say you must see her one last time. The people at the cremation center will strongly advise you not to see your mother like that. They say it will scar you for life to see her that way, that you should remember her nicely. Well, little did they know the horror you lived with and how you were already scarred. You will be brave, tough forty-one-year-old Grace, and you will walk into the incinerator room, trembling with fear, with guilt, elation, curiosity. Your abuser, your own mother, your wretched and also beloved mother, is finally dead.*

*You will look at her in awe. She looks so peaceful now. There is no more pain, no more anger in her face. Even with her black and blue zombie skin that is falling off her bones, she looks so peaceful.*

*You will stare at the big mole on her forehead. Looking at her mole as she lies dead on the table will trigger a flow of memories for you. You used to stare at that mole every bloody day when she used to scream at you for hours and hours. You knew every single detail, curve and shade of that mole.*

*And now the mole is dead.*

*THE MOLE IS DEAD. HOLY SHIT, YOUR MOTHER IS DEAD.*

*And now you can finally live your life. You knew as a child this day would come, and it does.*

*Forty-one-year-old Gracey, the time that follows will be the next important chapter of your healing. You will learn every day how to forgive yourself. You will begin to understand you truly cannot forgive others without forgiving yourself first. With that forgiveness, you will find gratitude. Gratitude for the pain and the suffering because it helped manifest a new Grace. Grace with meaning in her life.*

*You will begin to help people who have suffered like you. You begin to realise your story isn't that unique. So many people in the world can identify with so many different aspects of your story. We are all human and we all suffer from pain. You will begin to understand this is what bonds us, through our human challenges and how we triumph over them, and how we help others with the lessons we have learnt from our own healing journeys. Our unique pains and stories bring collective healing and transformation to the world.*

*Gracey, you begin to realise the final stages of your own healing is using what has happened to you to help others. And this is your path. You will help people learn how to eat, be healthy, release addictions, live with joy, have more energy, alleviate depression and anxieties, help others learn to love themselves. You will help people with your knowledge because you have been though it yourself. You know it authentically, from the depths of your heart.*

*And it will become so clear to you, sweet forty-seven-year-old Gracey, this is why you were born. This is the meaning of your life. You were meant to go through all this pain and suffering, and you were meant to triumph over it. And everything you learnt about overcoming your challenges and pain, you were meant to share with the world. This is why you were put on this earth,* to help others overcome their own suffering. Your own healing brings healing to others. You will help thousands and thousands of people improve their health and their lives. You will travel the world teaching people how to eat and live with self-love and compassion. You will teach people how to harness their own freedom and power through their lifestyles and reprogramming their brains. You will teach people how they can even heal disease by changing their diet and lifestyle. You will give people hope, inspiration, and strength; the strength that has always been inside of you since you were a little girl. That strength will help others access their own strength. You will help change people's lives and futures time and time again. And that will feel good. That will feel so right! All the pain you endured suddenly become worth it because you can transfer that pain into helping others. There was meaning behind all of it, Gracey. Your pain has become such a gift for the world. Your "mess" has become your message.

It will become so clear this is the meaning of your life; to heal and to love, and to teach others the same. Healing and connection within oneself brings healing and connection to others, and ultimately the world.

And none of this would ever be possible without your wretched, beloved mother. And you will begin to feel such gratitude and love for this woman who taught you how to truly live.

**What golden nuggets did you learn from your experience?**
I have learnt that anything and everything is possible, that you can change your brain and thoughts, you can love and trust again and learn to open your heart, that forgiveness is possible. I have learnt you can go from extreme self-hatred to a place of love, contentment, inner peace, and even joy. It is possible. I have lived it.

I have learnt we are all stronger than we think we are. I have learnt the negative thoughts we repeat in our minds are usually not ours and have been imposed on us as children by adults around us. As conscious adults, it is our duty to break the cycle of negativity that does not serve us as adults. We are not responsible for the programming we picked up as children, but we are 100 per cent responsible for fixing it as adults.

I have learnt that when you learn to love yourself, your whole world changes.

**What would you tell other women who might be experiencing this?**
You matter. Your life matters.

You are enough, exactly as you are, right now, today.

Open your eyes and you will find love all around you.

**What are some of the things you would have changed about your situation if you could?**
Nothing. Through this exact chain of events, I am where I am today. I wouldn't change a thing. I am who I am today because of everything

I have gone through. I am grateful for my life and all the people I get to affect because of who I am and where I've been.

**Any final words?**
Don't give up on yourself. Ever. Keep trying always. Stay dedicated to your path of truth.

Your current reality reflects how much you love yourself.

When you are ready to get real with yourself, the universe will always support you. Angels will always appear to help you on your path. Angels might not be who you think they are. Stay open.

Follow your joy. Let that guide you.

**How can people get in touch with you and see the work you do?**
I am the creator and founder of GLO Self-Care Center in northern Nicaragua. This place was birthed to support people in their journeys of self-care and self-love. We teach all aspects of health and lifestyle, with a strong focus on anti-inflammatory, plant-based, fresh food therapy, and movement in nature.

My international schedule is here: *www.gracevanberkum.com*
GLO Self-Care Center schedule is here: *www.graciouslivingoasis.com*

You can also find my posts daily on FB and Instagram:
*@GraceVanBerkum (IG) @GraciousLivingLifestyle (FB)*

"Trust that you are perfect as you are. Do more of what makes you happy. Seek a balance between being there for everyone and being on your own. Please stay close to your heart and follow your intuition. Listen to the little nudges from within and above. And take the steps that show themselves."

– Antonia Daniek –

# First Go Within – Then Join to Win

**Antonia Daniek**

*Changemakers Impact Strategist, Speaker, Visionary,
Founder of the Changemakers Impact Circle, Author of the
book JoinToWin*

What are you passionate about and how are you contributing to the world?

I am passionate about people supporting each other, collaborating and sharing their talents. I deeply believe we all have something precious to bring into this world, and that we can – as soon as we understand who we truly are – create a peaceful, healthy world together.

During my life journey and while working as a mentor and coach, I discovered how essential it is to know your own power and be true to who you are. Only then you can be a powerful part of a community and connect with others without fear and feelings of competition. Just imagine, if people mastered being able to fully be and choose themselves, listen to their intuition and understand how to collaborate with others, how different this world would be. This is what I am all about.

By empowering people to connect to their inner source and higher vision, I support them to see their big picture, tap into their intuition, collaborate freely and create positive change in their life and business. I kindle the spirit of co-creation and unity.

**Describe a pivotal moment in your life you wish to share.**
To understand the pivotal moments in my life, it is good to know where I come from. Growing up in a Buddhist community, I have experienced deep connection within a group, and at the same time, the value of everybody being unique and accepted as they are, combined with a deep wish to create a better world for all of us, by humbly being the best version of ourselves.

I have ten pivotal moments, and each led to the next, adding up to a chain of precious insights.

No 1: A night filled with fire, when I experienced that people don't necessarily work together, especially in the face of fear.

No 2: Understanding what true collaboration looks like when we did the school play.

No 3: Moving into a Buddhist community, discovering my international heart.

No 4: When I quit art school and changed my studies – so my mind was no longer bored.

No 5: When my mom was diagnosed with cancer and I had to decide whether I would stay in India discovering my heritage or go home to be with her, and what that meant to me.

No 6: When I ended a relationship to fully dive into discovering who I truly am.

No 7: When I took a leap of faith and put my career at stake – when I quit everything without knowing what would come next and was rewarded with a miracle.

No 8: When I invited my best friends to a creative weekend and it changed my professional future.

No 9: When I was reminded of how essential it was to take good care of myself, especially during the months when my husband was deployed.

No 10: When I grew my business from home and acknowledged my wish for more international work – and I reached out for help – and together we made it happen.

**Looking back, what made it such a pivotal part of your journey?**
All those moments marked either precious insights or decisions that changed my life, some even in a drastic way. They show a variety of times of self-discovery, connection and collaboration, of deep trust into life and into my intuition. They all build on each other. They are my golden thread; they co-create the way of life I truly love.

Based on the wealth of knowledge, wisdom and experience you have now, what would you like to say to yourself back then?

*Dear Antonia, my beloved one,*

*I would like to share with you some stories about your life, to encourage you to trust that everything happens for a reason.*

*Very soon, you will be at a New Year party with your mom at a friend's house. You will have a lot of fun that night. But at one point your mom will see the Christmas tree is starting to burn, because one candle has burned down to the bottom and set the tree alight because the needles are dry. Your mom will yell that the tree is burning – but no one will listen. You will be in shock, as you can feel your mom's fear and your own. But please stay calm. Everything will be okay.*

*It will happen very quickly. Suddenly the whole tree is ablaze, and then everybody in the room will notice. Finally, they will believe your mom.*

*When all the curtains are alight, they will curl up and fall like dust. People will panic and rush towards the door. But someone has pulled the keys out of the lock and the door is locked. So they will have to test every key on the big bunch while more people are panicking.*

*But not your mom. She will be the one to stay calm, the one to take you to the bedroom, where the air is fresh, without smoke.*

In that room you will both wait until this chaotic, uncoordinated group finally manages to open the door and everyone can leave.

You will recall from this moment people not working together, the acting without thinking and all the adults running around fighting for their own safety. I can happily tell you this event will be one of a few moments in your life where you experience people not working together.

Six months on, you will have a magnificent experience in your school, when all the kids come together to create the yearly school play. With your friends you will write the storyline and create all the characters. Each of you will have your own unique figure. The paralysed boy in your class will have a role where he can lie on the floor and another child will lie down beside him. You will create all the scenery and some parts of the stage will only exist in your mind. Together you will create anything you want, even a huge ship with three masts, and the audience will see it in their imagination as well, because you all see it so vividly.

You will all go on an extraordinary adventure. You will discover the treasure chamber of Pharaoh Tut-Anch-Amun. In this moment, in that imaginary cave, you will experience the pure joy of being on an adventure and having great success while working together, each individual in their uniqueness, accepting each other as they are. You will keep this memory as a valuable treasure for years to come.

*A year later, your life will shift and feel unstable because your parents will decide to separate, but don't worry, they will stay friends and co-parent. You will have a choice where you want to live, and your father will always be in reach.*

*Shortly after their separation, your mother will find Buddhism as her spiritual home and she will have the dream of creating a Buddhist retreat centre with her new boyfriend. They will make their dream come true and, soon after, you will all move to a beautiful house on a hill, together with your brother, mom and several friends.*

*Your whole life will change, from living in the city with your small family of four, to living in the countryside with a community of people from different backgrounds, ages and cultures. Now you live in a commune with joyful evenings of celebration, peaceful retreat weekends and a lot of international guests. It will be a completely different life. And you will love it. This is the birth of your international heart, of you being a world citizen.*

*The people in the retreat centre have a common Buddhist mindset, a way to approach life, open-minded and working together towards benefiting others. They see karma as part of their being; they are responsible for what happens to them.*

*They will believe that we all have a Buddha nature within us, so everyone is already perfect, we just need to discover ourselves. We just need to let go of what holds us back, of the old habits and the illusion we still have in our minds.*

*This mindset and lifestyle is so YOU; you will enjoy having it all around you.*

*Eventually your father and his new wife will move close by so you can visit them often and play with their little son. You will even be at their house, when your sister is being born. You will cherish this sacred moment filled with awe about the wonders of life.*

*As much as you enjoy the community, you sometimes prefer to be in a small family. This you will find with your father and your boyfriend's family. You will always have both.*

*In your final year of high school, you will have a fun time with a crazy bunch of friends. Together you will create the yearbook and organise the big celebration for the last day of school. You will work many nights on these projects, creating amazing pieces of art and entertainment, always bringing people together, communicating, designing and organising.*

*As you love graphic design, you will go to art school in Hamburg, with your beloved boyfriend studying in the same city. At the beginning you will enjoy the studies, but after three months you will discover that pure graphic design is boring. In high school, your two main subjects were art and maths. Now you're sitting there drawing and your brain is on standby. You cannot imagine this to be the profession of your future.*

*So, you will decide to finish the term and do something else. You wish to stay in Hamburg to be an intern at a graphic design* company, to see what they actually do, but you don't have a plan of how to get an internship. Here, the solution will come in an unexpected way. At the Christmas celebration in your art school, you will share your ideas of internship with a friend of your teacher. He will listen and keep asking questions. And at one point, early in the morning, he will tell you he owns a design company and they were going to advertise on Monday for an intern, and you have saved him the effort. So, by chance, you will tell the right person about your dreams and they will hire you.

You will have six months of creative work with two amazing people, mainly doing work for medical companies. You will enjoy experiencing the real work of graphic designers. With one of the customers, you will be in every meeting with the product manager. Even though you are just the intern, you have a full voice, your ideas are heard, and several are being produced.

At this point, you understand something precious about your life: you are a lot more interested in why things are created within a company than how the ads will look. This helps you to understand that business management and marketing will be your next study topics. There you can use your brain and be a creative force within the company vision.

But you decide that, before you continue with your studies, you will take a six-month break, fulfilling an old dream of yours, to travel alone to India to study Tibetan Buddhist philosophy and language in New Delhi.

*Just before you leave for this trip, you will talk to your mom and your father's wife about the idea of studying economics while doing an apprenticeship. You wish to be part-time in a company and in university, so you will have the real-life experience while studying. Your father's wife, who runs her own organic essential oil company, will tell you her new sales director has just told her he wants to have an apprentice and, if you want, it can be you. You can start as soon as you are back.*

*Sitting in the plane to India, you will understand something essential about the power of choice and taking action. As you sit there looking out the window, you contemplate that, within hours, you will be in a completely different culture on a faraway continent. Six months in a totally new life. And all it took to make it happen was to book this one flight.*

*In India you will have a trip of a lifetime, diving deep into your Buddhist heritage and making friends across the globe. Unfortunately, while you are there, you're going to be faced with a really hard decision, as your mom's going to be diagnosed with cancer.*

*What you choose to do in that moment is to stay, and I can tell you that, even though you might feel guilt and fear, it's the right decision. It will enable you to discover insights about who you are, and it will give you the opportunity to take part in the big welcoming ceremony of the Young 17th Karmapa Trinley Thaje Dorje, the reincarnation of your mother's teacher, the 16th Gyalwa Karmapa. You will be so happy you stayed.*

*Several months after you get home, you will marry your boyfriend. Even though you are still not living together, you will co-create a new life, shaping it between his profession as a soldier and your education as a future marketing expert.*

*The next years will be filled with studying and a creative mix at work. You will have something for your brain, for your creativity, for your organising skills and you will work with people. You love this range of topics and responsibilities.*

*Then your mother's illness will come back, this time painful and fierce. When this moment comes, please, breathe deeply and appreciate life, one day at a time.*

*Please accept how it is and remember how you prayed, ever since you were small. Remember your wishes that everything will be to the best of all beings. And that everything will come as it should. Please trust that it will be so.*

*Your father's wife will offer up her guest room for your mom. As you are living in the same house, you will be able to take care of her together. Your mother will appreciate this a lot and feel secure and safe. As she gets weaker, she will express her fear of being alone when she dies. From that moment on, twenty-four hours a day, someone will sit beside her bed. It will be you, your brother, father, his wife, your grandfather and good friends, each taking shifts by her side.*

*Your grandmother will stay at home and support by meditating and praying, powerfully enhancing the lineage of spiritual women in your family. Yes, you have strong female ancestors, way back to your great grandmother, who studied the Vedic wisdom in 1900. Each of these women went on her own spiritual path, and allowed the next generation to choose for themselves. Your whole family is spiritual in different ways, appreciating each other as they are. You are blessed.*

*The moment after your mom leaves her body, surrounded by family and friends, will be a sacred moment. You will feel love and relief: "Yes, she made it! She's better now."*

*In the following weeks, you will have your final exams and re-evaluate your situation. Now you have witnessed death, life somehow becomes more precious, and should have purpose.*

*But the purpose of your own life is not yet clear to you. You will start thinking about what you really want and realise the relationship with your husband has changed – something is missing. Actually, it's you who is missing, as you don't really know yourself. When you met, you were only seventeen and you had not figured it out yet. So now you will ask: "Who am I, outside this relationship? How do I want to live? How will I go on?"*

*Your heart will cry, because you love him and, at the same time, you will feel clearly that you cannot continue like this, because you don't know who you are.*

*So, you will separate; it will be painful and sad, but necessary, and he will move out quickly.*

*You will continue your life, find your way into work and start new studies.*

*Later, you will have a new boyfriend and improve in your job. You will explore what you really love and how you want to live. And, interestingly enough, it will be a lot like you had lived before with your husband, but in a new version. You definitely love to follow your intuition and travel without planning. You love spirituality, creativity, nature and being with friends. You are a gypsy in your soul. But with this boyfriend, you cannot live your gypsy nor your Buddhist life. You somehow need to hide parts of yourself and be an actress, and you do not like this. You will decide to be true to who you are, let go of this relationship and be alone.*

*This starts a big shift within yourself. You will realise you are hitting a glass ceiling with your work in this company and the village where you live is getting too small. You know it's time to move out into the world, and you will trust this feeling.*

*You will decide to leave at Christmas, without any idea where it will lead. This will bring miracles into your life which go beyond anything you could dream of. You will act as the next steps show themselves, and everywhere you go you will talk to people and look for signs towards those. For four months, no signs will show. And you will go on, patiently trusting, and that's perfect.*

*While you keep going, you will discover an interesting inner talk between your head and your heart. Regularly your heart will speak, requesting that you need to talk to your ex-husband, and your brain will answer that you're crazy, that you have left him and he's disappointed and hurt. It tells you to forget him. And yet, your heart will continue: "Please! Only once more. Talk to him once more, and then I will shut up."*

*This little nudge from your heart will always be there. But not strong enough for you to act. Well, your brain is really smart and persuasive.*

*Then there will be a strong nudge, with perfect timing. As you are preparing for an evening out with friends, you will suddenly have this impulse: "Now you have to call him! NOW!" It's a clear message from within or from above, and you will follow it and call him.*

*You will both be surprised when you hear each other. This is a blessed moment. You will talk for one hour and make an appointment for the next day to continue the call. That next evening, you will talk the whole night, about everything. You will tell him what happened after you broke up, about your boyfriend in between, about what you are up to now, and he will tell you his version. You will continue until six o'clock in the morning, when you both go back to work. And miracles over miracles; the next day he will have a holiday, and come to your place. You will restart a life together, a life that is both new and old, but with one big difference: now you know who you are. This will include your free spirit, your spiritual background and your inner strength. You know how you want to live, and that fits his lifestyle, and you know how to handle this whole situation and how to take care of yourself.*

*You clearly know you love him. The love for him was always there, but both of you needed those three years apart, to come back together. There is even no need for you to give up a job, or where you live, to be with him. You have already chosen this path of change for yourself.*

*So you will get married a second time to the same man, then the kids will come. Oh, yes, you will have three wonderful kids together. They will be happy, healthy children and your husband will provide for all of you, so that you can be there for the kids and later explore your professional future.*

*When your youngest son is two years old, you will invite your best friends for an experiential, creative weekend. It will be a great experience, because the five of you will each swap between teaching the others and being participants. So, part of the time, you will lead, and part of the time you will follow. And the whole time you will hold the space for this meeting. There you will discover a new version of how you love to work, and what you want to create in the future. Once more you will gain an important insight by following your intuition and inviting your best friends, so they meet each other.*

*This will be the starting point for your own coaching and consulting company. You will create spaces for growth, for groups and for intensive coaching, bringing people together, supporting them to discover what they want, and how they want to pursue it. You will show them new perspectives and encourage them to use opportunities, to create communities and to work together.*

*You will add several coaching educations to your portfolio and grow your business from there, step by step, while also taking care of your three children.*

*During some intense times with your family, like when your husband is deployed for seven months in 2013, you will manage to hold the energy for yourself and the children. You will feel that he's following his soul's journey while doing his work.*

*At one point, when you feel the pressure of responsibility for everything becoming too strong, you will create yourself a bright goal, like a guiding star. That year, you will book a flight to Sydney, Australia, for the following autumn. Knowing those two weeks will be just yours will give you the energy to keep going on. Two years later, you will go on another trip, this time to Phoenix, Arizona, where you'll connect to the land and to the indigenous people, and see the Grand Canyon.*

*You will understand it's important for your health and your inner peace to have this as an outlook, a space for being on your own, meeting people, learning and exploring, so you will regularly nurture your soul and heart with times in nature and travels. And then you are happy to be back.*

*Spending a lot of time with your family will always be a high priority for you, that's why you will choose to work mainly from home. You will grow your business while balancing between being there for everyone and taking care of yourself.*

*By working with business clients on a personal level, helping them to dive deep and see what difference they really want to make, you will support and encourage them to connect to their inner source and create from within, to take care of who they are and strengthen their source, like you are doing it for yourself. You will help them to see their bigger picture and themselves within it, opening their mind for co-creation and collaboration, and at the same time supporting them to walk their talk and bring their gold into this world, deeply trusting that they are perfect as they are.*

*Over the years, your connections will grow and you feel the urge to do more international work and to write your first book in English. To take this leap, you will look for mentors and inspiring groups, and they will support you to spread your wings. Together you will make it happen!*

*Your book, JoinToWin, will kindle the spirit of collaboration and be an inspiration to many people.*

*Thank you for taking this journey. You are precious.*

*I love you my darling. I am so proud of you.*

*With all my Heart, Antonia*

## What golden nuggets did you learn from your experience?

- Sometimes, it just takes one decision or one conscious action, and a lot of things change.

- Every time, when I dared to share my dreams, I was blessed with miracles.
- The moment you decide to set yourself free and let go, you open up possibilities.
- You can have BOTH – your own small family and your global tribe. You can take time for yourself AND have time for others.
- Trusting my intuition again and again, even though people did not understand or approve, like quitting my job with no idea where to go, is one of the best habits I created for myself.
- I feel my deep love for working with people and I am amazed at what we can create when we support each other.

**What would you tell other women who might be experiencing this?**
- Trust that you are perfect as you are.
- Make more of what makes you happy.
- Seek a balance between being there for everyone and being on your own.
- Please stay close to your heart and follow your intuition. Listen to the little nudges from within and above, and take the steps that show themselves.
- Explore the bigger picture of where you are, in the family, community and alone, and of where you want to go. It will help you create the life you dream of.
- Take time to discover who you truly are and what you want to do.
- Talk about your dreams.
- Always be true to yourself. It makes life worth living and brings unconditional love.
- Don't sit and endure unpleasant or toxic situations. No matter what others think or say: DO something about it. And when you

feel the leap is too big or the challenge too fierce, please go and get support. You DO NOT have to do it alone.

- Trust that you are always at the right time, at the right place with the right people.
- Dare to share the gifts you love to contribute and have the impact you love to have.
- I truly believe in you! If you have a shadow of a doubt in yourself, please feel free to borrow some belief from me. You are precious!

**What are some of the things you would have changed?**
Nothing – I am complete.

**Any final words?**
We will make a great difference in this world, one by one and all together.

**How can people get in touch with you and see the work you do?**
- Website: *https://www.AntoniaDaniek.com*
- Email: *connect@AntoniaDaniek.com*
- Facebook: *https://www.facebook.com/AntoniaDaniek.global/*

The book, **JoinToWin**: *https://www.jointowin.antoniadaniek.com*
Also available on Amazon.

# Special Thanks

When putting together a book such as this, it is never done alone. So many people are in the background, helping, supporting and encouraging along the journey. So this is a good place to thank so many.

Firstly, to the amazing, courageous and phenomenal authors, who not only stepped forward, but also overcame fears, trepidations and their own beliefs about their stories. Many of these women have not written in their mother language, but a secondary language, and I think it is a credit to them to step forward and have the faith that language is no barrier to touching the hearts and minds of others.

Secondly, to the amazing Marci Shimoff, who reached out a hand from the other side of the world and took the time to write a beautiful foreword to support us on our mission to touch one billion lives worldwide, even though she herself had such a busy schedule.

To the phenomenal support and help from Danni Blechner and her team at Conscious Dreams Publishing – *www.consciousdreams publishing.com* – for making this process so easy and painless – here's to many more books published by you.

Last, but not least, to my own family and friends; you know who you are. Thank you for your support, encouragement and for your constant belief in me and the work I do – I couldn't do it without you.

# Our Chosen Charity

With each *Pay It Forward* book, we support charities with a percentage of our profits and this book is supporting the following, heart-centred charity:

## Morijana
*Clothing That Changes Lives*

Morijana works with women who previously had little access to opportunities for self- empowerment, who face exploitation, such as street recyclers, garment factory workers and those living in slum communities.

As an ethical fashion business based in Phnom Penh, Cambodia, they work to develop, mentor and empower Cambodian women to realise their full potential. Each woman receives ongoing leadership, mentoring and training in design and all aspects of sewing, as well as health education and childcare.

All their clothes are made, pattern-designed and managed by Cambodian women, creating pants, shorts and tops in linen, cotton and 100 per cent viscose.

They operate with an open-plan workspace, fair wages and incentives.

To find out more about the clothes and the wonderful work they do, follow this link: *https://morijana.com/*

Printed in Great Britain
by Amazon

36258302R00185